Designing Online Experiments for the Social Sciences

Giuseppe A. Veltri

Designing Online Experiments for the Social Sciences

Los Angeles | London | New Delhi
Singapore | Washington DC | Melbourne

SAGE Publications Ltd
1 Oliver's Yard
55 City Road
London EC1Y 1SP

SAGE Publications Inc.
2455 Teller Road
Thousand Oaks, California 91320

SAGE Publications India Pvt Ltd
B 1/I 1 Mohan Cooperative Industrial Area
Mathura Road
New Delhi 110 044

SAGE Publications Asia-Pacific Pte Ltd
3 Church Street
#10-04 Samsung Hub
Singapore 049483

Library of Congress Control Number: 2022946358

British Library Cataloguing in Publication data

A catalogue record for this book is available from the British Library

Editor: Jai Seaman
Editorial assistant: Rhiannon Holt
Production editor: Nicola Marshall
Copyeditor: Christobel Colleen Hopman
Proofreader: Benny Willy Stephen
Indexer: TNQ Technologies
Marketing manager: Ben Griffin-Sherwood
Cover design: Shaun Mercier
Typeset by: TNQ Technologies
Printed in the UK

ISBN 978-1-5297-2504-9
ISBN 978-1-5297-2503-2 (pbk)

TABLE OF CONTENTS

TABLE OF FIGURES AND TABLES

Figures

Tables

ONLINE RESOURCES

Designing Online Experiments for Social Sciences is supported by a wealth of online resources for lecturers to aid study and support teaching, which are available at **http://study.sagepub.com/Veltri**

For lecturers

- **Additional Case Studies** to provide you with further examples to use in class or help bring theory to life.
- **Checklists** for each stage of experimental design to tick off key points of doing research and to ensure every step is considered.
- **Further Reading** at the end of each chapter you will find a suggested list of books and journals to help you explore topics further.

To the loving memory of my mother, Lia

ABOUT THE AUTHOR

 **Giuseppe Alessandro Veltri** holds an MSc in Social Research Methods from the Methodology Department of the London School of Economics (LSE) and a PhD in Social Psychology from the LSE. He is a Full Professor of Computational Social Science and Cognitive Sociology at the Department of Sociology and Social Research of the University of Trento, Italy. He was Senior Lecturer at the University of Leicester. He has been a Lecturer at the University of East Anglia and a scientific fellow at the European Commission JRC Institute for Prospective Technological Studies (IPTS). Before joining the IPTS, he has been a research associate at the Institut Jean Nicod (Ecole Normale Supérieure) in Paris. His research interests are in developing research methodologies of a computational nature for the social sciences and the intersection between sociology and behavioural sciences in the form of cognitive sociology.

He has published in scientific journals such as *Nature, Science Advances, Nature Scientific Reports, PLOS One, Computers in Human Behavior, Public Understanding of Science, Big Data & Society, Behavioural Public Policy* and others.

ACKNOWLEDGEMENTS

This book was written during a challenging time. The pandemic has hit Italy hard; we have seen loved ones pass away and everyday life disappear in front of the need to contain the pandemic. Universities and academics adapted the best they could. Still, it has been surreal and difficult to transfer all our activities online, limiting the opportunity to meet other people, students and scholars who enrich our work so much. Therefore, the academic work has been hectic because of the need to constantly keep adapting to the fast-moving circumstances of the COVID-19 pandemic. In this context, I would like to thank the Department of Sociology and Social Research of the University of Trento for being an environment that helps and stimulates research. It is something that academics cannot take for granted these days. Between video calls and online lectures, students have continued to be a source of stimulation. I particularly thank the students from the course of Computational Social Science for the degree in Data Science at the University of Trento. Likewise, I have been honoured to coordinate my department's PhD programme in sociology for the past two years. Reviewing and listening to the work done by the excellent young scholars of our small community has been another source of inspiration and insights.

In addition, I would like to thank people with whom discussions and work on online experiments have been continuous and stimulating: George Gaskell, Cristiano Codagnone, Francesco Bogliacino, Mauro Martinelli, Valentina Nerino, Filippo Andrei, Andrea Mammone, Nick Allum, Scott Wright, Shaojing Sun, Flaminio Squazzoni, Leo Kim, Ivano Bison, Mario Diani, Giuseppe Sciortino, Federico Neresini, Matteo Galizzi, Barbara Fasolo, Janina Steinert, Henrike

Sternberg, Yousri Mazrouki and many others that I will not be able to name all.

I also thank the great editorial team at SAGE Publishing, Jai Seaman, who helped start this project and Rhiannon Holt, who supported me in completing it. I have grown up as a student reading the research methods book by SAGE. Completing this book has been special compared to previous ones.

The last thank you and the most important to me is to my mother, Lia, who passed away while writing this book. The memory of her love, passion, curiosity and resilience are also in these pages through my work.

INTRODUCTION

The initial emergence of experiments followed on the heels of several technological advances. For example, the advent of computer-assisted telephone interviewing facilitated the implementation of phone-based survey experiments. The pace of technological change has accelerated even more in recent years. The costs and logistical challenges of data collection have dramatically dropped, enabling researchers to access survey and behavioural data at a notably larger scale. In recent years, four aspects of technological innovation have contributed to the diffusion of experiments among social scientists of all disciplines.

The first innovation was the increased easiness and reduced cost of obtaining data, thanks to the Web, the emergence of crowdsourcing platforms and the creation of an industry of commercial online survey panels. At the same time, the sharing of data across researchers has never been easier, thanks to the use of online public data repositories such as Dataverse, OSF or GitHub.

The second aspect was the emergence of social media which offered access to behavioural data and the opportunity to intervene experimentally. While using social media data for research is not without risks and ethical issues, it nevertheless prompted a new wave of studies in which experiments played a major role. The third element of innovation has been the diffusion of digital devices such as smartphones, tablets and portable computers to a large segment of the population in many countries. It allowed the deployment of survey and lablike treatments in field settings diminishing drastically the logical problems and costs.

All these advances in data collection have been accompanied by the diffusion of an increased computing capacity available to researchers at little cost and the development of new analytical methods to deal with complex and high-dimensional data.

However, while all these four innovations made it possible to carry out experiments on a large scale and of increasing complexity while reducing costs, it is probably a shift in research culture currently in place that created the conditions for the increased popularity of experiments. The social sciences have become increasingly attuned to the challenges of accumulating knowledge, given perverse incentives to exaggerate the size and statistical significance of treatment effects or, conversely, to bury weak or unexpected findings. The now-popular call for open science has highlighted the necessity of standards of transparency, pre-registration of studies and analysis plans, of incentives for replication.

The increased popularity of experiments is, therefore, characterized by the new availability of data sources and forms of collection, the introduction of new measurement techniques and the development of novel experimental designs combined with advancements in statistical methods. Conducting and publishing experiments is much easier than it was a few decades ago, and there are novel issues to consider (e.g. new sampling possibilities, design options and open science considerations).

The opportunities for conducting experiments have expanded to the point that we now witness the emergence of mega-studies in which large numbers of interventions are trialled in a single domain (e.g. Milkman et al., 2021, tested 53 different interventions to increase gym attendance against a control). The reasons for this type of study are both theoretical and empirical. The theoretical reason is related to the necessity of selecting the right interventions, a process that in previous times would have required a long cumulative process of trial and error based on smaller studies. By testing many interventions in a common context, the mega-studies provide a method to filter the most effective interventions.

The nature of data from this new generation of experiments is high dimensional because they are collected using multiple different sources, with different frequencies, over a long period of time and on a large scale. Using computational methods derived from computer science and statistical learning is increasingly common to analyze such experimental data. Therefore, another major source of innovation is the combination of experimental data with computational social science methods. In this book, we will discuss an application of what this merging can lead to, in particular focussing on how it can help researchers in terms of fully exploring the heterogeneity of treatment effects in large-scale experiments. Moreover, the role of prediction and machine learning techniques to achieve it represents a complementary part for the researcher involved in experimentation.

In the social sciences, the increased popularity of experiments is also due to a renovated debate on causality and social scientific research. For example, according to Watts (2014), most sociological research has privileged explainability over true detection of causality, relying on often common sense-based rationalization. However, while most social scientists are still at odds with the idea of embedding prediction in their quest to determine causality, as Watts (2014) argues, together with Woodward (2003), 'it is sufficient to assert only that when sociologists claim to have explained something, the clear implication – if not the explicit assertion – is that it satisfies a somewhat weaker "manipulationist" criterion for causality, meaning that it answers what Woodward (2005, p. 11) calls "a what-if-things-had-been-different question: the explanation must enable us to see what sort of difference it would have made for the explanandum if the factors cited in the explanans had been different in various possible ways"'.

In that respect, Woodward goes even further, arguing that, in fact, to state that if a proposed explanation does not pass this manipulationist test, then it is not an explanation at all but is mere description or storytelling.

In this context of renovated interest in experiments and causality by social scientists, this book aims at presenting the role of online experiments, with their specific strengths and weaknesses, as a valid, increasingly more sophisticated but accessible way of doing experiments for social scientists, particularly those that are not very familiar with lab experiments. Sociologists, political scientists, economists and, of course, psychologists are the natural readership for this book but also computer scientists who use experiments using different terminology (e.g. A/B testing). In computer science, the use of experiments that include social, economic and psychological dimensions is increasing, and the dialogue can be difficult as the word experiment has assumed the role of an umbrella term that summarizes different forms of experimentation.

This book focusses on what has become the predominant, or it appears to be, form of online experiments in the social sciences: the combination of online samples of participants with the use of platforms to deliver both stimuli and questions in a hybrid format. We discuss this type of online experiment in Chapter 1 of this volume. The use of online experiments needs to be discussed also in ethical terms. This topic is increasingly complex and continuously evolving. Hence, the account that this book provides is limited but, hopefully, useful to learning and considering the most important issues at stake. Chapter 2 of this book is dedicated to the ethics of online experiments.

In Chapter 3, we present the building blocks of experimental thinking, concepts like random assignment, and the basic design principles of experiments are inescapable learning aspects for all interested in any form of experiments.

The next part, Chapter 4, deals with the aspects of sampling that are specific to the type of online experiments we are focussing on in this book. As most social scientists are crucially interested in the external validity of their findings, online experiments need to be carried out using representative samples of the target population. Moreover, the possibility of deploying the same experiment across different countries or parts of a country requires careful consideration of the online panel of participants in different settings.

Chapter 5 presents several design issues concerning the interfaces and the vast range of different types of data that platforms can collect. We start discussing some graphical aspects of online experiments to conclude that it is somewhat the new frontier, the use of smartphones and their sensors to carry out experiments that are a hybrid form of online and on the field.

Chapter 6 focusses on the analysis part, considering the issues of attrition and non-compliance. Both are potential problems in the execution of any experiment, and to a certain extent, attrition is less common in the type of online experiments that we will discuss; however, non-compliance is important. In this book, we focus on one-sided non-compliance, the most common case. Two-sided non-compliance is also something to consider, but the complete treatment of the non-compliance issues is outside the scope of this book, mainly because it has already been extensively treated in many books about experimental design and analysis.

Chapter 7 provides some examples of types of experiments that are commonly carried out online. It is not an exhaustive list simply because the range of what is possible to do on online platforms is continuously being updated. The cases presented are not mutually exclusive in the sense they can, and have been, combined together in complex experimental design. For example, a framing experiment can be combined with a vignette or choice experiment. Ultimately, it is the researcher's goals, imagination and skills that will create new examples of what is possible to do in online experiments.

The last section is about a number of final considerations, both on encouraging social scientists to engage with online experiments and also looking at what the future might hold for this methodology. The digitalization of data collection and most of our daily lives and the rise of data science have created momentum for social scientists that has the potential to revolutionize the way how we do social science. There are risks and hypes, but it is undeniable that the new expectations for increased transparency, sharing of data and pre-registration combined with more stringent ways of considering causality claims are of great benefit to social science research.

At the same time, as in the example of online experiments, the role of social scientists remains crucial in understanding social phenomena, even with an abundance of data and always the new possibility of data collection. It is social scientists' responsibility to engage with the sources of these data, from social media platforms to the new industry of online opinion mining research.

This book is part of a new wave of texts that are trying to capture these changes in the way social scientists will do their research. Its focus is on online experiments and, in particular, the type of online experiments that the author has directly experienced. This text should be considered in combination with other books indicted at the end of each chapter complement provides a comprehensive view of the field of experiments in the social sciences and their latest innovation.

No single volume can account for all the potential applications in the social sciences of the new methodologies that are being developed. In a previous volume concerning digital social research (Veltri, 2019), the goal was to discuss the overall major innovation in social scientific methods like the potential of natural language processing and text mining, online qualitative research methods, the use of social media data and the others. The topic of online experiments, although present and briefly discussed, required a dedicated book and, very likely, the same can be said about the other forms of digital social research. And yet, online experiments appear to have a special place not only because of their potential to identify causal mechanisms but also because of their practical value in testing interventions. This book is one of the few, the most recent at the moment of this writing, dedicated specifically to online experiments and, hopefully, it will help social scientists and practitioners alike to see the potential of this way of doing research.

1

ONLINE POPULATION-BASED SURVEY EXPERIMENTS

- Highlighting the main differences between observational and experimental studies in the social sciences
- Explaining the internal–external validity debate about experiments in the social sciences
- Introducing the main features of online population-based survey experiments

- Regularity vs manipulability theories of causation.
- Internal validity is the approximate truth of the inference or knowledge claim made with respect to a particular target population.
- External validity refers to the generalizability of findings from a study or the extent to which conclusions can be applied across different populations or situations.

(Continued)

- • Population-based survey experiments are experiments conducted online that apply the sampling methods developed in survey design to achieve high external validity.

1.1 Observational versus experimental methods

The use of experiments in the social sciences has a long history. Some disciplines employ this methodology more often than others, for example, psychology. Still, since the end of the last century, their application has become widespread in other domains, like economics, political science and sociology.

Before describing the features of online experiments, it is helpful to discuss the issue of causation in the social sciences briefly. Hundreds of books and articles have been written on this topic, and the possibility of causally explained social phenomena is fiercely debated. Some do not believe it to be possible (e.g. Martin, 2011), and others do (e.g. Woodward, 2000). It is impossible to recount such a debate fully, and it is not among the aims of this book. Still, we need to be clear about one distinction between forms of causality to understand the difference between experiments and other methods.

In the social sciences, we have two separate forms of understanding causality: *regularity theories of causation* and *manipulability theories of causation*. Regularity theories are based on a long philosophical tradition that can be traced to David Hume and that defines causality as determined by temporal priority (the cause must precede the effect), spatiotemporal contiguity (cause and effect are near in time and space) and constant conjunction (if the same circumstances are repeated, the same outcome will occur). The tradition stemming from this position on causality has focussed on distinguishing between causal and non-causal relationships between variables (e.g. Simon, 1954; Yule, 1896). Starting with Hume, regularity theories of causation have been concerned with the full (or philosophical) cause of an effect, by which is meant a set of conditions that is sufficient (or necessary, or necessary and sufficient) for the effect to occur. The further elaboration of probabilistic causation in the regularity theories led to the development of concepts like 'spurious relationships'[1] and mediation effects between variables. Granger causation, a concept based on prediction, and structural equation models use this type of reasoning to distinguish between causal and non-causal empirical relationships. One of the implications of the regularity approach to causation is the need to specify all the variables and the functional relationship between these and the outcome one. Analysis done with survey data or other sources of quantitative information are analyzed using this approach to causality.

Experiments are, however, grounded on a different tradition of understanding causality: manipulability theories. This approach views causes as variables that can be manipulated, with an outcome that depends on the state of the manipulated variable. Rather than accounting for the relationships between several variables, including mediating ones, so as to reach an outcome, the goal is to examine the effect of a particular variable. It is not impossible to reconcile these two approaches, regularity and manipulability (Sobel, 1995). Manipulability theories require the causal relation to sustain a counterfactual conditional statement (e.g. eating the poison caused Mark to die; had he not eaten it, he would not have died). There are problems with this approach to causality too, particularity in terms of counterfactual theories (see their critique in Martin, 2011).

Experiments are therefore situated in a manipulability understanding of causality and their design is characterized by three main aspects: (1) manipulation of one or more independent variables; (2) use of controls such as randomly assigning participants to treatment or experimental or control groups and (3) careful observation and measurement of one or more dependent variables. An experimental

---

[1]In statistics, "In investigating spurious correlation we are in whether the relation between two variables persists or disappears when we introduce a third variable." (Simon, 1954, p. 469). In this relationship, multiple events or variables lack a causal link, but it might be mistakenly assumed they possess one due to coincidence or an undisclosed third element, known as a 'common response variable,' 'confounding factor,' or 'lurking variable.'

design identifies the independent, dependent and nuisance variables and indicates the way in which the randomization and statistical aspects of an experiment are to be carried out. The primary goal of an experimental design is to establish a causal connection between the independent and dependent variables. A secondary goal is to extract the maximum amount of information with the minimum expenditure of resources. Next, we consider two crucial concepts for understanding the logic of experiments that are particularly relevant for their web version: the notions of internal and external validity.

1.2 The internal–external validity debate

Crucial to any experimental design is the balance between internal and external validity. A randomized experiment presents an ideal opportunity for having (1) the data-generating process (DGP) of the variable of intervention subject to exogenous variation; (2) the participants to the study representative of the population object of the intervention; and (3) the behaviour measured in the lab (on average) identical to the variable of interests that we want to study with respect to our theory and/or the underlying real environment phenomenon of interest. The main strategic challenge is that experiments may remain a very 'local' type of evidence, and this is problematic if our goal is to support policymakers who are interested in general results. In fact, all the literature on experimental validity, as well as on internal and external validity, originated in the theory that Campbell and his associates developed on how to move from 'local' evidence to 'generalization'. The problem was framed as one of extension to other populations and settings (external validity) and of representation and measurement (construct validity). As noted (McGraw and Hoekstra, 1994; Shadish et al., 2002), in this effort, Campbell early on abandoned the single binary distinction between internal and external validity; first, Cook and Campbell (1979) extended the notion of internal validity and, later (see Shadish et al., 2002), he incorporated clarifications advanced by Cronbach with his UTOS (units, treatments, observation operations, settings) framework (Campbell, 1957); validity was divided into four concepts: causal validity, construct validity, statistical validity and external validity. In addition is ecological validity, which, as we shall see, partially overlaps with both construct validity and external validity, although it has its own distinct tradition in psychology, starting with Brunswik's (1943) suggestion that we should study the participant's setting, and is then further developed, particularly from an ecological perspective. In the sections that follow, I will describe the key aspects of different dimensions of validity, before briefly illustrating the main threats to validity. I will conclude with an analysis of trade-offs and of the different traditions and research purposes that explain the choices made with respect to them.

1.2.1 Internal validity

If validity in general is the approximate truth of the inference or knowledge claim, then internal validity is the approximate truth of the inference or knowledge claim made with respect to a particular target population. Following the same general definition, external validity would be the approximate truth of the inference or knowledge claim for observations beyond the target population studied.

Originally, Campbell (1957) considered an experiment internally valid if the experimenter finds a significant difference between the treatment and control conditions. These differences are then assumed to provide a meaningful reflection of the causal processes at play. As long as no reason exists to assume that some extraneous mediating factor systematically influenced participants' responses, observers can attribute changes in the dependent variable to systematic manipulations across the independent variables. From this perspective, internal validity is enhanced by experiments that are well designed, carefully controlled and meticulously measured, so that alternative explanations for the phenomena under consideration can be excluded. Shadish et al. (2002) are careful to note that internally valid findings remain discrete to the specific experimental context in which they are explored. As we have seen, Campbell and associates divided internal validity into three separate concepts: causal validity, construct validity and statistical validity.

Causal validity determines whether the relationships found by the researcher within the target population analyzed are causal. Establishing causal validity for the relationship between X and Y would mean establishing that changes in X cause changes in Y. Very often this is what analysts have in mind when they consider internal validity, whereas establishing a causal relation does not exhaust the criteria for assessing the internal validity of an experiment, if we recall that the goals are those of extension from local to general knowledge and of representation. We can possibly demonstrate that X causes variations in Y and that there are no other factors influencing them and yet score poorly in internal validity if the inferences we draw are flawed, for instance, by the fact that the variables we measured do not represent well the variable either in the theory or in practice, which smoothly leads us to consider the next dimension: construct validity.

Construct validity has, first and foremost, to do with how valid the inferences of the data are for the theory (or constructs) the researcher is evaluating (we discussed this issue in general terms in the first chapter). In experimental research, the question is whether the design of the experiment is such that the variables investigated are closely equivalent to the variables the theory is concerned with. Are those things that the theory holds constant held constant in the experiment? Are the choices before the participants the same as the choices assumed in the theory? In other words, is there a close match between what the theory (the real world) is about and what is happening in the manipulated DGP? As the theory can be assumed to deal with what happens in the real world, then the above sentences can to some extent be rephrased in terms of the adherence between the experiment and what happens in practice; for instance, are the choices before the participants the same (or similar enough) as the choices they face in the real world? In this respect, construct validity and ecological validity overlap, and the former is not immune from consideration in the trade-off between 'mundane' and 'experimental' realism (see below). So, although construct validity is a dimension of internal validity, construct validity is also about generalization and reflects the attempt to move from the local to the general by way of ensuring valid representation. Results from experiments with high construct validity can help us answer more general questions than those without construct validity.

Statistical validity, in simple terms, depends on the significance of the statistical relation estimated for the variables of interest and on the size of such a relation. Given the assumption made, and other aspects of the design and of the DGP, one must ask whether estimates are efficient, accurate, significant and sizeable and also whether the dataset is representative of the target population. Usually, other aspects of validity are considered more challenging and given more attention than statistical validity, as the latter is, so to speak, 'commoditized' given the increasing capacities of statistical software packages. Yet, there are questions that statistical packages do not solve and on which the research must reflect. What in general are the implications of different levels of statistical significance? What if we find a relationship that is just on the edge of the 5% level? Also important is the extent to which the assumptions about variables distribution are supported and whether or not errors are correctly estimated.

Mundane versus experimental realism. As argued by Aronson et al. (1990), despite efforts to prove otherwise, internal validity remains intrinsically tied to experimental, as opposed to mundane, realism. Those who are sceptical about the experimental method often point to the artificial nature of laboratory settings as a main weakness and an obstacle to generalization. The critique holds that tasks presented to participants offer a poor analogy to the real-world experiences that individuals confront. Strong proponents of the experimental method, especially in economic game-theoretic experiments, but also to some extent in psychology, argue on the contrary that stylized and stripped-down settings are needed to carefully operationalize and measure the variables of interest and then, through multiple tests on numerous populations, to begin to define the conditions under which generality might obtain. The reason it becomes so critical to uncover these mechanisms is that unless an investigator knows the underlying principles operating in a given dynamic, it will prove simply impossible to ascertain which aspect of behaviour is causing which effect within the context of real-world settings, where many other variables and interactions occur simultaneously. In this tradition, it does not matter whether the experimental environment does not overtly mimic the real-world setting, as long as the subject experiences the relevant forces that the investigator seeks to elicit. A more balanced view is to recognize that, if experimental participants become psychologically disengaged in the process, they confront and do not pay attention to performing the tasks and this clearly undermines internal validity and the possibility of extending the findings. If participants approach a task with scepticism or detachment, then genuine responses fade and strategic incentives come to the fore. This raises the possibility that measures obtained do not accurately reflect the process being manipulated but, rather, manifest a different underlying construct altogether. This is a clear threat to construct validity. Hence, the motivation of the participants and the internal experience of the experiment for them should ensure engagement, and for this to occur, the settings need not necessarily reflect outside appearances. The success of the experiment depends on the subject taking the task seriously, and experimenters can foster such engagement to the degree that they can create and establish a situation that forces psychological investment on the part of participants. The critical operative feature in such experimental designs revolves around the ability of the experimenter to create a psychological situation that realistically elicits the dynamics under consideration. So, experimental realism remains more important than mundane realism in maximizing prospects for internal validity because it is more likely to elicit the critical dynamic under investigation, but more highly stylized or abstract experimental protocols can risk both internal and external validity by failing to engage participants' attention or interest.

1.2.2 External validity

External validity refers to the generalizability of findings from a study or the extent to which conclusions can be applied across different populations or situations; too often, however, external validity is simply intended as a matter of representativeness or of the size of the sample. Privileging external validity often results from a misunderstanding that generalizability can result from a single study as long as it is large enough or broad enough; this is never true. External validity results primarily and eventually from replication of particular experiments across diverse populations and different settings, using a variety of methods and measures. As Aronson et al. put it: *'No matter how similar or dissimilar the experimental context is to a real-life situation, it is still only one context: we cannot know how far the results will generalize to other contexts unless we carry on an integrated program of systematic replication'* (1990, p. 77). External validity is the extent to which the *'causal relationship holds over variations in persons, settings, treatments, and outcomes'* (Shadish et al., 2002, p. 83). Hence, it covers four aspects of experimental design: (1) whether the participants resemble the actors who are ordinarily confronted with these stimuli; (2) whether the context (including the time) within which actors operate resembles the context (and time) of interest; (3) whether the stimulus used in the study resembles the stimulus of interest in the world; and (4) whether the outcome measures resemble the actual outcomes of theoretical or practical interest. So, the challenge for external validity is to extend to other participants (i.e. representativeness *sensu stricto*), other observations, other treatments and other settings as in the UTOS framework articulated by Cronbach (1982) for establishing valid causal inference. Finally, it is worth pointing out that, often, when critics say that an experiment does not have external validity, they just have in mind that the sample used (in the laboratory) is not randomly drawn; yet, this has to do with internal statistical validity and not with external validity. Random sampling from a target population does not necessarily mean that a result is externally valid. External validity has to do with generalizing to populations beyond the target population, so whether one has a random sample from the target population tells nothing about the external validity for other populations for which one has not taken a random sample.

With each innovation comes the requirement to ensure that the methods reveal what they claim they do. For Web research, there seem to be two primary ways to establish validity: (1) compare results from a web-based study with a laboratory-based study and (2) examine the research to see if the results follow theoretically predicted trends. Web experiments may be used to validate results from field research and from laboratory experiment or they may be used for new investigations that could only be feasibly accomplished in this medium. Because many laboratory experiments are conducted on computers anyway, nothing is lost when an experiment is designed web-ready; it can always also be used in the laboratory. In distributed web experimenting, local collaborators recruit and assist participants who all log onto the same Internet-based experiment. External validity of web experiments may be limited by their dependence on computers and networks. Also, many studies cannot be done on the web. However, where comparable, results from web and laboratory studies are often identical (Reips, 2002a).

1.2.3 Ecological validity

As a starting point, ecological validity can be seen as referring to the relation between real-world phenomena and the investigation of these phenomena in experimental contexts. Yet, as for other dimension of validity, there are many different definitions (Scheidt, 1981, pp. 225–226). The focus on ecological validity started with Brunswik's (1943) suggestion to study the participant's setting. It then continued with Bronfenbrenner's (1977) echoing of the same emphasis and with Neisser (1976) arguing that the stimulus materials should be ecologically valid. In brief, ecological validity concerns focussed on the realism of three aspects: the settings, the stimuli and the responses. Ecological validity involves maintaining the integrity of the real-life situation in the experimental context while remaining faithful to the larger social and cultural context. More intuitively, ecological validity is similar to what Harrison and List (2004) refer to as the 'fieldness' of an experiment.

Ecological validity is a dimension that could be considered as a subset of both external validity and construct validity. If we consider it in terms of settings (the S in Cronbach's UTOS framework), then obviously ecological validity is a subdimension of external validity. However, if we look at ecological validity as concerning the problems that may arise from the interaction between the aseptic (artificial) context typical of a laboratory experiment and the behaviour of participants, which means the interaction between the design and the measurement of the variable of interest, then lack of ecological validity can actually be seen as a problem of construct validity inasmuch as the measurement generated may not validly measure the underlying construct (phenomenon) because, for instance, of participants' disengagement with the experimental task. It is about the similarity between the environment constructed in the research and a target environment. Some experimentalists call this mundane experimental realism or contextual congruence. The experimental environment is considered ecologically valid if the methods, materials and settings of the research are similar to the target environment.

It must be clarified, however, that maximizing ecological validity may or may not enhance external validity of the results because it may not be possible to generalize the target environment. External validity can be conjectured or hypothesized based on similar studies or assumptions about population similarities concerning any study, experimental or non-experimental, but the proof of external validity is always empirical.

1.2.4 Main threats to validity

Campbell and Stanley (1966) identified nine threats to internal validity that may lie outside the experimenter's ability to control: selection, history, maturation, repeated testing, instrumentation, regression towards the mean, mortality (attrition), experimenter bias and selection–maturation interaction. Below, we consider only the most important of these.

Non-compliance can be active or passive and may occur in different forms; one is when those assigned to the treatment group do not receive the treatment, or when those assigned to the control group inadvertently receive the treatment. In this case, the randomly assigned groups remain comparable, but the difference in their average outcomes measures the effect of the experimental assignment rather than actually receiving the treatment. Another form of non-compliance is disengagement that is more subtle but as serious as active or passive forms of non-compliance. Many standard forms of analysis assume that everyone who receives treatment experiences a similar level of engagement with the protocol, but this assumption is often faulty because non-compliance rates can be non-trivial. Non-compliance raises the prospect of artificially inducing treatment values into the estimated outcome effects. If participants are not paying attention or are thinking about something unrelated to the task at hand, then it will remain unclear whether the manipulation actually exerted an effect.

Attrition involves the failure to measure outcomes for certain participants (e.g. some do not report their vote preference in the follow-up) and is particularly problematic when it afflicts some experimental groups more than others. Attrition occurs when participants drop out of an experiment or are otherwise lost to follow-up. This only poses a threat to internal validity to the extent that it occurs subsequent to random assignment (Kiesler et al., 1969). If participants drop out prior to such an assignment, then it may constitute a threat to the external validity of the experiment (sample characteristics), but not to the internal validity of its findings. However, if participants in one condition are dropping out of an experiment at a higher rate than those in another condition, then it may be that such attrition is in fact effected by the treatment itself.

Experimental effects (or, in experimental economics, experimenter demand effects) refer to the way in which people change their behaviour simply because they know they are being monitored. Participants may get from the situation or directly from the experimenter cues about what constitutes appropriate behaviour and act accordingly or against it. They are usually a potential problem only when they are positively correlated with the true experimental objectives' predictions, and we identify techniques such as non-deceptive obfuscation to minimize this correlation. Harrison and List (2004) argued that manipulation by an experimenter puts participants on an 'artificial margin' and may lead participants to alter their behaviour on unconstrained margins. There are different types of effects; in psychology, they have been classified precisely (Howitt and Cramer, 2011, pp. 202–206). One particularly important subclass is referred to as the 'experimenter expectant effect' when, unintentionally, the researcher convinces participants to act or behave in a particular way in order to achieve what the experimenter wants. Another such subclass is known as 'demand characteristics', which occurs when participants influenced by the experimental situation (that gives cues to the hypothesis) alter how they act.

A different source of effects potentially undermining validity is the so-called 'experimental cross-effect' that can occur (1) when participants' choices in an experiment are influenced by the manipulations they have received in previous and distinct experiments or (2) when participants' choices in one task of a given experiment are influenced by the manipulations they have received in a previous task of the same experiment. This threat is particularly relevant in within-participants designs, where it can be the source of order and learning effects, and increases the other experimental effects cited earlier, including social desirability and hypotheses guessing.

Restricted sample and selection bias. Restricted subject populations can also limit the degree of potential generalizability from studies, although the degree to which this problem poses a serious threat varies with the topic under investigation. Although it is generally better to have more participants across a wider demographic range, depending on the content of the study, it may be more important to obtain more participants, rather than explicitly diverse ones. Selection bias, in terms of non-random sampling, represents another threat to external validity that also threatens internal validity. If participants are drawn from too restrictive a sample or an unrepresentative sample, then obviously more replication will be required to generalize the results with confidence.

1.2.5 Trade-offs between different forms of validity

Obviously, it is best to strive to maximize both internal and external validity, but this may run counter to practical and logistical constraints. Maximizing internal validity may diminish the ability to extrapolate the findings to situations and populations outside those specifically studied. Privileging external validity often neglects important aspects of internal experimental control so that the true cause of reported findings remains unclear. Two principal trade-offs exist between internal and external validity. Attention to internal validity optimizes the ability of an investigator to achieve confidence that changes in the dependent variables truly resulted from the manipulation of the independent variable. In other words, methodological and theoretical clarity emerge from careful and conscientious documentation of variables and measures. In contrast, concentration on external validity by expanding subject size or representativeness can increase confidence in generalizability, but only to the extent that extraneous or confounding hypotheses can be eliminated or excluded from contention. Regardless of the solutions adopted, the trade-off will always remain between the ability to control and measure carefully defined variables and testing in more realistic settings for the purpose of ecological and external validity. External validity and the capacity to extend from the local to the general remains legitimate, but it is a concern that should arise only after prior sufficient attention is given to internal validity first. As argued by Aronson et al.: *'Internal validity is, of course, the more important, for if random or systematic error makes it impossible for the experimenter even to draw any conclusions from the experiment, the question of the generality of these conclusions never arises'* (1990, p. 75). A single very large (in terms of sample) and very contextually rich and realistic experiment will never ensure external validity as such. External validity will come with replication across time, treatments, populations and settings.

Having said this, differences in the extent to which researchers give more priority to one or the other dimension of validity remain and depend on the disciplinary tradition and/or the purpose for which experiments are carried out. Disciplines such as political science and sociology have been slow to adopt the experimental method; they are more concerned with generalization than, for instance, psychology and experimental/behavioural economics. Whereas in political science and sociology the concerns with external validity are at times excessive, the reverse is true for psychology and experimental economics with their priority on internal validity. The purpose of the experiment, not always coinciding with the disciplinary tradition, also plays a role. If the goal of the experiment is to extend theoretical models or data generation, then internal validity is the priority, especially in game-theoretic experiments undertaken by experimental economist stylization and aseptic settings, which are sought for the sake of internal validity. However, if the purpose of an experiment is to support policymaking, then external validity tends to have at least as much importance as internal validity because policymakers are interested in the potential extension of results to large and different populations and settings. And, yet again, it is important to remind ourselves that striving for external validity at the cost of internal validity will not make the evidence base of policymaking any better. We can quote again Aronson et al.:

> Bringing the research out of the laboratory does not necessarily make it more generalizable or 'true'; it simply makes it different. The question of which method is – 'artificial' laboratory experiments versus experiments conducted in the real world – will provide the more generalizable results is simply the wrong question. The generalizability of any research finding is limited. This limitation can be explicated only by systematically testing the robustness of research results across different empirical realizations of both the independent and dependent variables via systematic replication to test the extent to which different translations of abstract concepts into concrete realizations yield similar results. (1990, p. 82)

In conclusion, the very concrete purpose of the experiment will shape the needed balance between internal and external validity. Exploring a fairly universal human experience (i.e. some very basic emotional reaction through visual stimuli for instance), it is very unlikely that college students will differ from other population groups and even from college students from other countries. In other situations, external validity will instead require having a broader sample in terms of representation of different sociodemographic segments.

1.3 Population-based survey experiments

The limitations of online laboratory experiments and the opportunities as a field in which to conduct research have prompted researchers to develop online experiments both in academia and in the private research world.

Of particular interest is the form of online experiments that combine lessons learned from online surveys. The aim of the so-called 'population-based survey experiments' (PBSEs) is to address this problem through research design rather than analysis, combining the best aspects of both approaches, capitalizing on their strengths and eliminating many of their weaknesses. The aim of this volume is to introduce social science scholars and students to the possibilities of this approach.

Defined in the most rudimentary terms, a PBSE is an experiment that is administered to a representative sample of the population. Another common term for this approach is simply 'survey experiment', but this abbreviated form can be misleading because it is not always clear what is meant by the term 'survey'. The use of survey methods does not distinguish this approach from other combinations of survey and experimental methods. After all, many experiments already involve survey methods at least in the administration of pre-test and post-test questionnaires, but this is not what is meant here. PBSEs are not defined by their use of interview techniques, whether written or oral, nor by their location in a setting other than a laboratory. Instead, a population-based experiment uses *sampling* methods to produce a set of experimental participants that is representative of the target population of interest for a particular theory, whether that population is a country, a state, an ethnic group or some other subgroup. The population represented by the sample should be representative of the population to which the researcher intends to extend his results. In PBSEs, experimental participants are randomly assigned to conditions by the researcher, and treatments are administered as in any other experiment. But participants are generally not required to show up in a laboratory to participate. Theoretically, we suppose they could, but population-based experiments are infinitely more practical when representative samples are not required to show up in one place.

To further clarify, for the purposes of this volume, when we use the term 'experiment' in the context of PBSEs, we are referring to studies in which the researcher controls the random assignment of participants to variations in the independent variable in order to observe their effects on a dependent variable. It is important to note that the term 'experiment' is often used much more broadly than this particular definition. For example, many classical 'experiments' such as Galileo's observation of gravitational acceleration do not involve the random assignment of conditions. And in the social sciences, Milgram's famous demonstration of obedience to authority initially did not involve any second group or source of comparison, although he later added them to his design.

Thus, while there are many important experiments that do not meet this definition, we exclude these types of studies from my definition of PBSEs for two reasons. First, in order to be able to make clear statements about the contribution of population-based experiments to internal and external validity, we must limit the discussion to experiments for which these two ends are actually primary objectives. Establishing causality and generalizing to a defined reference population are not always the goals of research, but they are central to most social science work. Moreover, the type of experimentation we circumscribe is one in which PBSEs have the most to offer. Other types of experimental studies could undoubtedly benefit from more diverse subject populations, but since experiments that do not fall under this definition focus on other purposes, this methodological development is less important for these types of studies. However, when scholars want to be certain that a given relationship implies cause and effect, and that their theory can be generalized beyond a small group of participants, then this is precisely the context in which PBSEs can make their greatest contribution.

Strictly speaking, PBSEs are more experiments than surveys. By design, population-based experiments are experimental studies that draw on the power of random assignment to establish unbiased causal inferences. They are also administered to randomly selected representative samples of the target population of interest, just as a survey would be. However, population-based experiments do not need (and often have not relied on) nationally representative population samples. The population of interest could be members of a particular ethnic group, parents of children under 18 years, people who watch television news or some other group, but the key is that convenience samples are abandoned in favour of samples that represent the target population of interest.

The advantage of PBSEs is that theories can be tested on samples that are representative of the populations to which they are said to apply. The downside of this trade-off is that most researchers have little experience in administering experimental treatments outside of a laboratory setting, so new techniques and considerations come into play, as Veltri (2019) describes extensively.

In a sense, PBSEs are by no means new; simplified versions of them have existed since at least the early years of research. However, technological developments in survey research, combined with the development of innovative techniques in experimental design, have made highly complex and methodologically sophisticated population-based experiments increasingly accessible to social scientists from many disciplines. Unfortunately, apart from a few journal articles that have been written by early adopters of this technique, there has so far been no book that has addressed the subject in a comprehensive and accessible way.

Population-based experiments are not easily labelled. As a result, the guidelines available in textbooks for each of these individual methods – for example, internal and external validity considerations, design advice and so on – do not address the specific problems of population-based experiments. The aim of this volume is to fill this niche, and thus to encourage a wider and more informed use of this technique in the social sciences.

Why is the population-based experimental approach only now emerging as a distinct methodological option? Two technological innovations have led to the emergence of this method. The first was the development of computer-assisted telephone interviewing (CATI) technology. Until the development of CATI, there were strict constraints on experimental designs carried out in the context of large population samples. The classic 'split-ballot' experiment allowed for the variation of a single aspect, whereas current technologies allow for multiple variations of multiple factors. It is no longer necessary to produce many different versions of a paper questionnaire because the software simply does it for you, with the appropriate variation of the experimental stimulus appearing automatically on the interviewer's computer screen. This advance has enabled researchers to carry out extremely complex experimental designs on large and diverse groups of participants using telephone surveys.

In addition, the development of the Internet has further expanded the possibilities of population-based experiments. Although Internet interviews with representative samples of the population are still in their infancy, it is already possible to provide pictorial stimuli and films to random samples of respondents. The ability to exploit such dynamic data collection tools has expanded the methodological repertoire and inferential range of social scientists in many fields. Although PBSEs were done by telephone or face-to-face long before the Internet-based interview emerged, the Internet has greatly increased their potential.

The many advances in interview technology present social science with the potential to introduce some of its most important hypotheses into virtual laboratories scattered across the nation. Whether evaluating theoretical hypotheses, examining the robustness of laboratory results or testing empirical hypotheses of other varieties, the ability of scientists to experiment on large and diverse groups of participants allows them to address important social and behavioural phenomena more effectively and efficiently.

Population-based experiments can be and have been used by social scientists in sociology, political science, psychology, economics, cognitive science, law, public health, communication and public policy, to name but a few of the main fields that find this approach interesting. But the list does not end there. Population-based experiments have been used in more than 20 disciplines, including psychiatry, anthropology, business, demography, African American studies, medicine, computer science, Middle Eastern studies, education, history and even aviation studies. As long as the perceptions, behaviours or attitudes of human beings are of interest, and the researcher's goal is to test a causal proposition of some kind, PBSEs are probably valuable. But they are particularly so when the study is one that benefits from combining the internal validity of the experiments with the external validity of representative samples from the population.

Although most social scientists recognize the enormous benefits of experimentation, the traditional laboratory setting is not suitable for all important research questions, and experiments have always been more popular in some fields of social science than in others. To a large extent, the emphasis on experimental versus investigative methods reflects a field's emphasis on internal versus external validity, with fields such as psychology more oriented towards the former, and fields such as political science and sociology more oriented towards the latter.

Regardless of the field or emphasis of one's methodological training to date, PBSEs challenge us to expand our methodological repertoire and reconsider the 'truisms' about more traditional methods. For some researchers, survey methods are their primary means of data collection. However, there are often substantial obstacles to drawing strong causal inferences from conventional survey data. Over the years, many have hoped that advances in statistical methods would allow scholars to use survey data to check all plausible rival interpretations of a potentially causal relationship. But despite the massive and impressive advances in statistical methods over the years, few people today are optimistic that statistics can solve all our problems of causal inference. For survey researchers, population-based experiments provide a means of establishing causality that is unmatched by any large-scale data collection effort, no matter how extensive.

Experimenters arrive at population-based experiments with a different monkey on their back. Having solved the problem of causality in many areas of research by relying primarily, if not exclusively, on experiments, fields such as psychology are commonly accused of ignoring external validity. Can we really assume that the way sophomores in college work is the way all people work? Psychologists have made some good arguments for the generalizability of results in areas such as basic human perceptual processes. But they are less convincing when it comes to many other areas of knowledge where generational differences or life experiences come into play.

In an ideal world, researchers would not be identified by method, and we would all be experts in a variety of approaches. But since we are clearly not there yet, what is new and exciting in population-based experiments will vary for researchers in different fields. For this reason, we will sometimes risk redundancy in reviewing some basics so as not to take a particular reader too much for granted. The goal in this book is not to provide a resource for the basics of experimental design, nor to discuss the finer points of survey research methods, especially since there are much better sources on both of these topics. Instead, my aim is to stimulate the use of this approach by providing a sense of its potential and situating PBSEs in relation to experimental and survey research.

Throughout the natural and social sciences, researchers employ experimental designs to combat the challenges posed by the fundamental problem of causal inference. To review the problem in a nutshell, in order for one variable to be said to 'cause' another, three conditions must generally be met, the 'holy trinity' of causality: (1) the two must co-vary, both in time and across units of analysis; (2) the cause must precede the effect in time and (3) the relationship between the cause and the effect must not be explicable through some other third variable, which would make the association spurious. In practice, few scholars have problems establishing the first criterion, and the second is only problematic for studies based on cross-sectional observations where a plausible causal argument can be made for reverse causality.

Thus the 'third variable problem' is the key reason why experiments are known as the gold standard for inferring causality. Experiments are the best possible way to deal with the problem of third variables and potentially spurious relationships. This 'holy trinity' of causality is well known in the social sciences, but the third variable problem has been distinguished by a lack of robust approaches to solving it. For temporal precedence, researchers can use time series designs, but there is no parallel solution to the third variable problem. In observational research, omitted variable bias plagues or at least threatens most causal arguments, and there is no simple solution other than an experimental design.

Throughout the social sciences, experimental design strategies involve one of two approaches to the problem of causal inference. Researchers either (1) evaluate a unit of analysis before and after a given treatment compared with those evaluated before and after without treatment and then draw inferences from these pre-post within-subject comparisons or (2) use a between participants' design in which several participants are randomly assigned to groups receiving different experimental treatments, often including a control condition.

What is noteworthy is that one of these approaches, as well as much more complex experimental designs, is easily implemented in the context of surveys using computer-assisted telephone interview platforms or Internet-based interviews. The ability to make strong causal inferences has little to do with the laboratory environment itself, and much to do with the ability to control the random assignment of people to different experimental treatments. By moving the possibilities of experimentation out of the laboratory in this way, population-based experiments strengthen the internal validity of social science research and provide the potential to interest a much wider group of social scientists in the possibilities of experimentation. Of course, the fact that it can be done outside the laboratory is not in itself a good reason to do so. Therefore, below we will examine some of the key advantages of population-based experiments, starting with four advantages they have over traditional laboratory experiments, and then ending with some of their more general benefits for the accumulation of useful social scientific knowledge.

Table 1.1 provides a concise overview of the pros and cons of online experiments, where the laboratory experiment is the implicit benchmark. The main strategic advantage of an online experiment over a laboratory experiment is the greater possibility of generalization (external validity), greater statistical power and possibly the quality of the data produced. Web-based studies, having larger samples, usually have greater power than laboratory studies. Data quality can be defined by variable error, constant error,

Table 1.1 Pros and cons of online experiments

Pros	Cons
Wider access to sampling. Easier access to a large number of demographically and culturally diverse participants.	*Multiple presentations*. They can be avoided or controlled by collecting personal identification (evidence is that multiple presentations, however, are rare).
Generalizability/quality of data. Better basis for generalizing results to the general population and to more environments and situations (due to high external validity). Higher power and quality of data.	*Less experimental control*. Variability of the environment (lighting, noise, technical characteristics of the equipment used, e.g. type of browser, connection speed). In the absence of control by laboratory assistants, participants may give 'noisy' answers (given without paying attention). These problems are less important in inter-subjective designs with random distribution of participants to the experimental conditions.
Improved efficiency and logistics. The automation of experimental procedures reduces costs and increases the uniformity of the procedure among participants.	*Self-selection*. Only interested and motivated participants can start and complete the experiment. The use of the multi-site entry technique can reduce self-selection.
Detection of motivational confounding. See the opposite cell on abandonment.	*Dropout*. This is always a problem in web experiments. However, the dropout can be turned into a detection device for motivational confounding.
Reduction of experimenter effects and demand characteristics.	*Lack of interaction*. This may cause misunderstandings between the participants but can be avoided by pre-testing and pilot testing.

Sources: Batinic et al. (2002), Birnbaum (2004), Dandurand et al. (2008), Gosling and Johnson (2010), Reips (2000, 2002a, 2002b), Reips and Krantz (2010).

reliability or validity. Comparisons of power and some quality measures have found cases where web data are of higher quality for one or other of these definitions than comparable laboratory data, although not always (Birnbaum, 2004, p. 825). The question feature is a subtle clue that makes participants aware of what the experimenter expects to find or how participants are expected to behave. Question features can change the outcome of an experiment because participants often alter their behaviour to conform to the experimenter's expectations. Many web researchers are convinced that data obtained via the web can be 'better' than data obtained from students (Reips, 2000), despite the obvious advantage that the laboratory offers for control. The main disadvantage of an online experiment compared to a laboratory experiment is the lack of full environmental control. Participants in online experiments may answer questions and perform behavioural tasks in very different environments (a room with light and silence, versus their own desk at work with less light and surrounded by a lot of noise) and with different equipment (a participant may use a browser that does not properly display visual stimuli or may have a slow connection, thus delaying task completion and increasing fatigue, frustration and 'noisy' responses). Most importantly, as lab assistants do not monitor participants, there is more chance that they will engage in automatic responses and task completion, which introduces noise into the data. This can be controlled with control questions and is less of a problem for between-participants design with randomization of treatments and control conditions.

There are other technical/tactical issues that can be controlled in the online experiment (multiple submissions, drop-outs, self-selection – in effect, almost identical to what we have already discussed about web surveys), but the main trade-off between the online experiment and the laboratory is to trade off greater generalizability and power of the data for less experimental control. It is therefore not surprising that experiments are often repeated with the same outcome measures both online and in the laboratory to check the quality and validity of the data. Other advantages of online experiments are

- the speed of data collection and 24-hour testing,
- a high degree of automation of the experiment (low maintenance, limited experimenter effects) and
- a larger sample in terms of both size and wider geographical variation of participants.

Data collection techniques on the Internet can be grouped into *server-side* and *client-side* processing. Server-side methods (a web server, often in combination with a database application, serves up web pages that can be created dynamically depending on a user's input) are less prone to platform-dependent problems because dynamic procedures are executed on the server so that they are not subject to technical variations. Client-side methods use the processing power of the participants' computers. Therefore, time measurements do not contain errors due to network traffic, and server availability problems are less likely.

In terms of disadvantages, apart from the already mentioned problem of experimental control, there are other potential limitations that are evident depending on the research topic. These include the following factors:

- The dependence of web experiments on computers and networks with psychological, technical and methodological implications.
- From a cognitive point of view, computer participants are likely to be subject to self-actualization and other influences in computer-mediated communication.
- The time duration of online experiments is shorter than that of laboratory experiments.

This last point is related to the use of online panels for recruiting participants. In my experience, the problem of obtaining generalizable samples is becoming less of a concern due to the decreasing costs of pre-recruited online panels from the general population, although concerns about response rates remain (see the previous section on web surveys for further discussion on this topic). Online panels have different costs in terms of sample size and duration of the experimental task, the most common duration being about 20 minutes. Therefore, online experiments that include time-consuming tasks face two problems: higher costs and greater potential to reduce control over respondents. Although there is no clear evidence to support this claim, my general impression is that online experiments exert a greater cognitive toll on respondents than laboratory settings. The reason may be that it is easier to exercise concentration and attention in an environment designed to allow this – the laboratory – than in other settings, such as the home.

1.3.1 Online experiments as field experiments

So far we have discussed the characteristics of experiments with randomized controlled trials in mind as the standard, but online experiments can also take the form of field experiments (Centola, 2010; Goldstein and Hays, 2011; Hahl and Zuckerman, 2014; Ong and Wang, 2015; Parigi et al., 2017). Field experiments typically consider pools of participants from the general population acting under conditions, and making choices, in the real world. Participants are usually unaware that they are part of a social experiment until the end, thus minimizing the risk of observing behaviour distorted by the 'experimenter effect'. All this increases the external validity of experimental trials, while maintaining the ability to understand the effect of a target variable that is 'manipulated' (i.e. assigned to the treatment group and not assigned to the control group). Field experiments are indeed effective in gathering evidence about people's actual behaviour. In field experiments, people are directly observed in the actual context of their use rather than in abstract, stylized and perhaps distant-from-reality experimental tasks designed by researchers.

For example, in the commercial domain (e.g. e-commerce platform), it means that the experimenter can manipulate, one by one, the characteristics of the frame, context and other sales conditions within which products are normally sold (e.g. colours, position, sequence, order of presentation of information, offers, multi-item promotions). It is important that the field simulation allows researchers to assess not only the immediate reaction of consumers to minor or apparently unperceived changes in the sales context and setting but also general changes in consumer spending behaviour in shops or online. An example of an online field experiment is the study mentioned at the beginning of the introduction of this book, entitled 'Experimental evidence of massive-scale emotional contagion through social networks' (Kramer et al., 2014), in which the field was Facebook and its users (some of them) were the unwitting participants in an experiment to manipulate their emotional states. This example highlights both the scientific potential of a field experiment and also the ethical problems that can arise when the manipulation of thousands of individuals is involved.

The role of experiments in digital research is growing in large part because experiments are mainly conducted using computer-assisted tasks and because the first hurdles to obtaining representative samples are less problematic (though not entirely) using pre-screened online panels. This is true for experiments that have used the online as an alternative 'venue' to the laboratory. At the same time, experiments that deal with native online behaviour and social phenomena have appeared. These are field experiments where the field is digital. Questions about the ethical feasibility of these experiments have been raised with the realization that academic researchers are no longer alone (they probably never were) in using this methodology. Private research companies, as well as big tech ones, use experiments to test new features on their platform, running hundreds of field experiments a year to improve usability, prolong user interest and maintain sales rates. Outside of the academic ivory towers, it is very likely that we have all been part of such an experiment when using our digital platforms of choice.

1.4 Chapter summary

In this chapter, we have discussed the following points:

- We have highlighted the main differences between observational and experimental studies in the social sciences. We explained the approach of the manipulability approach to causation that is distinct from other approaches.

- We have explained the internal–external validity debate about experiments in the social sciences and how this issue has been an obstacle to adopting experiments in the wider spectrum of social science disciplines.
- Internal validity is the approximate truth of the inference or knowledge claim made concerning a particular target population.
- External validity refers to the generalizability of findings from a study or the extent to which conclusions can be applied across different populations or situations.
- We have introduced the main features of online PBSEs.

PBSEs are experiments conducted online that apply the sampling methods developed in survey design to achieve high external validity.

Further readings

There are several excellent texts out there for those interested in getting to know more about the opportunities and challenges of doing web surveys. Excellent books are: Tourangeau et al.'s (2013) *The Science of Web Surveys*; the more recent and very complete book by Callegaro et al. (2015), *Web Survey Methodology* and Bethlehem and Biffignandi's (2012) *Handbook of Web Surveys*.

Within this section, we have already referred to the excellent book on adaptive survey design by Schouten et al. (2017), *Adaptive Survey Design*, which describes adaptive approaches well suited to web surveys.

Moving to experiments, two recent texts come to mind: Druckman's *Experimental Thinking: A Primer on Social Science Experiments* (2022) and, in the field of industry and computer science, Kohavi, Tang and Xu's *Trustworthy Online Controlled Experiments: A Practical Guide to A/B Testing* (2020).

2

THE ETHICS OF ONLINE EXPERIMENTS

━━━━━ Chapter objectives ━━━━━

- To understand the difference between obtrusive and unobtrusive methods
- To place the role of informed consent in social scientific research using experiments
- To introduce the notions of minimal risk, deception and debriefing
- To recognize the nature of data according to their privacy aspects
- To problematize the issue of integrity of materials
- To understand the approach of avoiding harm in social scientific research

━━━━━ Key concepts ━━━━━

- Digital data vary in terms of how much active is the role of participants in the data collection process. Obtrusive methods require participants' active engagement with a researcher's data collection. Unobtrusive methods can be conducted without the active participation of the people producing or eliciting data.

(Continued)

- Informed consent is still the cornerstone of ethical conduct in social scientific research including the digital one.
- Minimal risk is assessed when informed consent cannot be collected. Minimal risk is a condition in which participants involved in an experiment will be exposed to information or task that are not different from what they could encounter in their everyday life without causing them harm.
- Concerning privacy, whenever full anonymization is not possible, recently the European General Data Protection Regulation (GDPR) has introduced the notion of pseudonymization, which is the processing of personal data in such a way that the data can no longer be attributed to a specific data subject without the use of additional information, as long as such additional information is kept separately and subject to technical and organizational measures to ensure non-attribution to an identified or identifiable individual.
- Social scientists must attempt to avoid and minimize harm to research participants. Many risks can be anticipated and minimized (e.g. confidentiality, invasion of privacy, drug treatment side effects).
- Social scientists are compelled to protect test integrity. If test items are widely available, some test takers might know the answers and be able to fake a high or low score.

2.1 Obtrusive and unobtrusive research online

Digital data vary in terms of how much active is the role of participants in the data collection process. In fact, we can distinguish digital data as the outcome of unobtrusive or obtrusive methods of data collection (Webb et al., 1966). Obtrusive methods require participants' active engagement with a researcher's data collection. Unobtrusive methods can be conducted without the active participation of the people producing or eliciting data. The distinction between these two modalities of data collection is important in the social sciences because people 'react' to researchers' measurements and also can figure out what a researcher's goals are. Two of the most common problems are generated by people's reactions to measurements, the Hawthorne effect and the social desirability effect. The Hawthorne effect, as mentioned before, refers to the fact that individuals modify their behaviour in response to their awareness of being observed. Recent scandals related to social media and privacy, in which users' data have been harvested for commercial or political campaigning purposes, have made people more conscious of the fact that their online behaviour is observed and recorded. Social desirability is the tendency of some respondents to report an answer in a way they deem to be more socially acceptable, if they believe are under observation, than would be their 'true' answer, where true means aligned to current dominant social norms. They do this to project a favourable image of themselves and to avoid receiving negative evaluations. The outcome of the strategy results in the overreporting of socially desirable behaviours or attitudes and the underreporting of socially undesirable behaviours or attitudes (Nederhof, 1985). Social media are particularly affected by social desirability bias because people manage their presence online in order to generate a positive self-image. This process leads to a positivity bias in the content present on social media (Spottswood and Hancock, 2016).

The distinction between obtrusive and unobtrusive methods is not new to digital social research. In the pre-digital age, surveys, interviews and focus groups were typical reactive data collection methods. At the same time, types of social scientific research like content analysis relied on documents that were produced 'distantly' from researchers.

Based on digital research methods (Veltri, 2019), the range of unobtrusive data collection methods has increased compared to the pre-digital past. Table 2.1 reports a classification of the most common digital research methods: surveys, interviews and experiments are all examples of reactive modes of collection. The analysis of online content in its various forms, both quantitative and qualitative, is instead a form of non-reactive data collection. Often, researchers can collect information about web pages without any required action from their owners, and the very same applies when we interface with a social media platform's gateway to its data, the so-called

Table 2.1 Online obtrusive and unobtrusive data collection methods

Researcher Presence	Quantitative	Qualitative
Obtrusive/reactive	Online surveys Online laboratory experiments	Online interviews Online focus groups Online field research
Unobtrusive/non-reactive	Quantitative web content analysis Social media network analysis Online field experiment Online natural experiments	Qualitative web content analysis

application programme interface (API) which defines the protocols to query a platform and its data.

It is precisely the increased opportunity of online unobtrusive methods that has generated concerns about the so-called *covert research*. Online research poses in general a risk to individual privacy and confidentiality because often methods prevent participants from knowing that their behaviours and communications are being observed and recorded (e.g. a large-scale analysis of postings and exchanges in a Usenet newsgroup archive and a chat room).

The diffusion of covert research methods has challenged the established practices of ethical evaluation adopted in most research institutions. The cornerstone of ethical conduct has been the notion of informed consent that is the procedure by which the researcher informs participants about the nature and risks of the study, being sure that these are fully understood and accepted before proceeding any further. While this practice has been transported to online obtrusive methods from offline procedures without too much trouble, the use of digital data of an unobtrusive nature has been more problematic. The key points about informed consent for these modes of data collection are to understand when and how informed consent can be secured. Context here does matter in the sense that we need to consider what information is being retrieved and how the information will be used. A common distinction made is between digital sources that are specifically designed to facilitate content production and sharing such as websites, blogs, microblogging and newsgroups. In contrast, those that are designed for social networking might or might not have expectations of public sharing content. A further complication is given by the fact that these are fast-moving targets, meaning that their options and settings are quickly evolving. Think, for example, about the possibility of sharing Facebook content with different 'publics' such as everyone, just your friends or a subset of them.

Most researchers have considered and treated the first type of sources as public even though some had terms of usage constraints (often not very explicit or visible). The line here has been blurred. Some content allows for 'fair use', agreed to by their copyright arrangement, and academic research has been often placed in this category because of its non-profit nature. However, simply assuming that these arrangements work for all sources is risky. The same expectation of 'fair use' cannot be said about social media data. While people are increasingly more aware of the public nature of their published and shared content, the platform is making their task more difficult and their exposure to third parties (such as apps within the platform) has increased (Stutzman et al., 2013).

The other challenging point is how to ask for informed consent when the datasets are vast and often longitudinal, meaning that data are collected retrospectively. For very large datasets, increasingly common in digital social research, the feasibility of obtaining consent from every single participant is challenged. Further complicating the overall picture are the mutating legal context and the differences between countries. The already mentioned European regulation, the General Data Protection Regulation (GDPR), on these matters requires informed consent every time data that have been collected for one explicit use are repurposed for another, a situation in which many researchers find themselves.

The debate about privacy (and ownership) of digital data is not going to end soon given that their nature is changing, and their pervasiveness is increasing. There are those who are persuaded that simply social norms about privacy have changed, and people care less as long as they receive in return valid services. However, the presence of a 'privacy paradox', according to which there is a gap between people's intentions to disclose online and actual levels of disclosure (Acquisti et al., 2015; Norberg et al., 2007; Veltri and Ivchenko, 2017), does lend support to this view. Overall, the distinction between obtrusive and unobtrusive data collection methods does not concern only strict methodological aspects, but a much wider discussion about the ethical implications of digital data research and, at the societal level, about social and legal norms of privacy and data ownership.

2.2 Personal data and privacy

From the initial stages of less privacy-aware use of APIs and digital data of citizens, much has changed. In 2018, EU countries adopted a new data privacy regulation: the GDPR.[1] While this regulation applies only to the European Union, it is setting the bar for many other countries and therefore it is of particular interest for academic researchers and worth exploring in a little more detail. A key point for academic research (and any type as well) is the regulation of *further processing*, which corresponds to what we have defined in this book as the 'repurposing' of data. In other words, data collected by one entity are passed to another actor that analyzes them. In the GDPR, research occupies a privileged position. Organizations that process personal data for research purposes may avoid restrictions on secondary processing and on processing sensitive categories of data (Article 6(4); Recital 50). As long as they implement *appropriate safeguards*, these organizations may also override a data subject's right to object to processing and to seek the erasure of personal data (Article 89). Additionally, the GDPR may permit organizations to process personal data for research purposes without the data subject's consent (Article 6(1)(f); Recitals 47, 157).

The first step for those who collect personal data is to obtain a lawful basis for any processing activity. Article 6(1) of the GDPR delineates the lawful bases for processing, which include the data

---

[1]The full GDPR regulation document is available at https://eur-lex.europa.eu/legal-content/EN/TXT/?qid=1532348683434&uri=CELEX:02016R0679-20160504.

subject's consent and processing that is necessary for the legitimate interests of the data controller (e.g. researchers). Where a controller collects personal data under a lawful basis, such as consent, Article 6(4) allows it to process the data for a secondary research purpose. However, the GDPR has introduced an exemption to the principle of purpose limitation for research. Article 5(1)(b) states: 'Further processing for archiving purposes in the public interest, scientific or historical research purposes or statistical purposes shall, in accordance with Article 89(1), not be considered to be incompatible with the initial purposes'. In other words, the GDPR clearly intends to relax restrictions on further processing personal data for research purposes of public interest. This creates a unique opportunity for academic researchers because it provides an incentive to businesses to partner up with institutions of public interest like universities. It also provides a partial solution to the issue of access, which we have already discussed, but it is premature to claim that this will be the case or that the regulation will create a different kind of relationship between the business sector and academia from what we see now.

The other important point introduced by the GDPR is a much higher emphasis on notification. Although data controllers are not required to obtain the data subject's consent for all processing for research purposes, they remain bound by the GDPR's notice requirements. Article 12(1) requires controllers to 'take appropriate measures' to inform data participants of the nature of the processing activities and the rights available to them. Data controllers are required to provide this information in all circumstances, regardless of whether consent is the basis for processing, 'in a concise, transparent, intelligible and easily accessible form, using clear and plain language' (Article 12(1)). Notification, given its new crucial role, is something that deserves more attention in the workflow of academic research.

As well as consent and notification as two of the cornerstones of the new European data protection regulation, the notion of proper safeguards is introduced, in Article 89. According to this article, the 'controllers' (of data) must put in place 'technical and organizational measures' to ensure that they process only the personal data necessary for research purposes, in accordance with the principle of data minimization outlined in Article 5(c). When processing personal data for research purposes, Recital 33 states that data controllers should act 'in keeping with recognized ethical standards for scientific research'. It is worth noting that, in the context of data research, as opposed to more traditional human subject research, those very ethical standards are still being debated. This debate at the policy-making level is one in which social scientists should play a bigger role. Article 89 introduces also the notion of 'pseudonymization', which is 'the processing of personal data in such a way that the data can no longer be attributed to a specific data subject without the use of additional information, as long as such additional information is kept separately and subject to technical and organizational measures to ensure non-attribution to an identified or identifiable individual'. Unlike anonymous data, pseudonymous data remain subject to the remit of the GDPR. Many of the techniques traditionally used to protect privacy in research settings, such as key coding, fall within the definition of pseudonymization and therefore remain subject to the GDPR. The difference between 'true anonymous data' and pseudo-ones will be another controversial issue.

2.3 Ethical regulatory guidelines

Online psychological research differs from in-person psychological research in many ways (Mathy et al., 2003), and many of these differences present challenges to designing an ethical study. The first obvious difference is that researchers usually have no direct contact with participants. Ethically, there are two benefits of lack of direct contact. It is easier to ensure complete anonymity, which may explain why online studies obtain higher response rates on sensitive questions (McCabe, 2004). And participants do not feel as much social pressure to stay, which increases their ability to discontinue participation if they become uncomfortable (Birnbaum, 2004b; Fricker and Schonlau, 2002; Kaplowitz et al., 2004).

Lack of direct contact does, however, present three challenges to designing an ethical study. First, researchers cannot use visual and verbal cues to determine whether participants understand the consent form and debriefing or are upset by their content. Second, researchers cannot provide immediate clarification if participants have questions about consent or debriefing. Third, researchers cannot easily verify that participants are legally old enough to consent. These challenges are not unique to online studies; they occur to various extents in mailed surveys, telephone surveys and group testing sessions.

We will provide practical advice addressing several ethical issues: informed consent, deception, debriefing, the right to withdraw, the integrity of test materials and avoiding harm.

2.3.1 Informed consent

When the researchers and participants have no direct contact, the researchers must design the consent process carefully to ensure that the participants understand the information given (Kraut et al., 2004; Mathy et al., 2003). We recommend that researchers use simpler language than they would during an in-person study and avoid idioms unless they know in advance that all potential participants will have high language fluency. In addition, if researchers are recruiting from a population that is likely to include people with disabilities, they should design their study materials to conform to World Wide Web Consortium Web Content Accessibility Initiative Guidelines (Web Content Accessibility Guidelines Working Group, 1994–2007), by incorporating such features as adjustable text size and text labels for all graphics.

A written signature is easily and routinely obtained in laboratory settings. Unfortunately, if signed documentation of consent is needed in an online study, this will be inconvenient because clicking on a button that says 'I consent' is not legally equivalent to a written signature. When documentation of consent is needed, we recommend that researchers continue to use paper signatures. Participants can print, sign and mail the consent form. Digital signatures can be legally substituted for written signatures; however, digital signatures are no more convenient than paper signatures when consent is documented because each individual using a digital signature first needs to prove his or her identity to the entity that grants the digital signature. Thus, digital signatures do not represent a viable alternative to paper consent forms at this time. For studies that are at minimal risk (in terms of potential harm to participants), we do have legally acceptable online documentation of consent. The picture is more complex when we deal with studies that are more than minimal risk where there is now a substitute to a paper and officially signed consent form. We recommend that researchers document consent (e.g. by including a no-consent option) whenever participants may have poor computer skills or below-average fluency in the language used. Children can assent to participate in research, but they cannot legally consent. Consent must come from their parents or legal guardians. Because researchers are not present in online studies, studies that require consent need to build a question-asking opportunity into the consent process. At a minimum, researchers must provide contact information before asking participants if they consent and must reply to questions in a timely manner. We recommend that additional question-asking opportunities be given if the study has more than minimal risk. First, we recommend that researchers make it easier for participants to ask questions. They could do this in at least two ways. The study could be available only when the researcher is available to answer questions, either by phone or in a chat room. Alternatively, participants could be asked to email the researcher to indicate that they consent and to ask any questions that they have before the researcher gives them access to the study materials. For studies involving more than minimal risk, we recommend that researchers take one additional step to ensure understanding: assess comprehension. Therefore, if a study involves more than minimal risk, we recommend that researchers embed questions about the process, benefits and risks of the study in the consent form, as has been suggested by Frankel and Siang (1999) and Stanton and Rogelberg (2001). If potential participants answer the questions incorrectly, they can be given additional information. Because web pages can dynamically interact with participants, ensuring participant comprehension may be easier in online studies than in some in-person studies (particularly group testing sessions).

There is also the situation of excluding adults who cannot consent. A variety of conditions can impair someone's decision-making capacity and thus impair their ability to consent to research. These include substance abuse disorders, mental retardation, dementia, schizophrenia and depression. The first approach is to avoid recruiting them. The second approach is to assess someone's capacity to provide informed consent; this may be necessary if researchers cannot rule out the possibility of recruiting people who may have impaired cognitive abilities.

2.3.2 Deception and debriefing

Next, we move on to the topic of deception. Here there is a disciplinary diversity about the possibility of employing deception in experimental studies. In economics, it is strictly ruled out. In psychological research, it is allowed in a mild form and with certain conditions. We will discuss the second option as the first one does not require further considerations. Deception may also be easier to justify if researchers ensure that almost everyone receives the debriefing. For example, researchers can ask participants for consent to minor deception or for consent to withhold some details about the study and can tell the participants that they will be fully debriefed at the end. This may increase the probability that the participants will read the debriefing, and we recommend that researchers use this technique whenever feasible.

In other words, if the study involves deception, explain the deception to participants during the debriefing. Researchers must take reasonable steps to correct participants' misconceptions and thus must take reasonable steps to ensure that all participants receive debriefing information (and understand it).

Debriefing is a crucial moment and it needs extra care in the context of online studies. For in-person studies, participants can ask their questions directly. However, online studies need to build in methods of obtaining additional information. This can be relatively easy. Researchers can provide contact information again at the end of the study and answer questions within a few days. Alternatively, researchers can provide answers to common questions at the end of the study. However, dropouts who close the browser window or who switch to another website will not read debriefing information that is given at the end of the study. Because dropout rates tend to be high in online studies, additional steps should be used if complete debriefing is important.

2.3.3 Withdraw

Withdrawing participation. Participants have the right to withdraw at any time. In person, participants may feel social pressure to continue participating because they want to be polite or researchers say that they need data. In contrast, participants feel little pressure to remain in online studies – an ethical advantage of online research (Reips, 1997, 2000).

Participants with poor computer skills may experience difficulty in withdrawing. They may not know how to exit by closing the window or using the address bar or back button. If some participants are likely to have poor computer skills, researchers should provide a simple method of withdrawing, such as 'Quit the study' links on each page. This is particularly important if participants must answer every question before the computer lets them submit their responses. For example, participants might be required to give contact information so they can receive research credit or payment, and in some studies, participants are required to answer every question, so that the researcher obtains complete data and scale scores are valid. Whenever participants are required to answer questions before they can submit their responses, participants who do not know how to exit a page on their own may feel compelled to answer questions that they do not want to answer. If such participants will be recruited for the study, a simple method of withdrawing should be provided as part of the study itself.

Withdrawing data. When participants withdraw, they may also want to withdraw their previous responses. Few ethical codes explicitly state whether the right to withdraw participation implies the right to withdraw previously submitted data. In our opinion, the importance of data withdrawal depends on the study and why the participants withdraw. If the participants withdraw because they no longer want to continue the experience (e.g. they are bored or fed up), allowing data withdrawal may not be important (and those participants may also be unlikely to read and answer questions about data withdrawal).

In a paper-based study, withdrawing data is simple: If a participant says that he or she wants to withdraw the data, the pieces of paper are simply shredded. In an online study, the researcher needs to build in methods of withdrawing the data. There are three methods of withdrawing data in an online study. First, if the data have not yet been submitted, a reset button can erase answers. Second, if the data have already been submitted, the participant can request that the data be withdrawn by answering a question about data withdrawal at the end of the section or the end of the study or by emailing the researcher. Third, with some database designs, the participant can remove the data from the database without the researcher ever seeing it. The participant answers a data withdrawal question, asking that the data be removed, and the database removes the data immediately. Whichever method is used, researchers should tell participants the consequences of withdrawing from the study, including the consequences of different methods of withdrawing.

2.3.4 Integrity of test materials

Social scientists are compelled to protect test integrity If test items are widely available, some test takers might know the answers and be able to fake a high or low score. To reduce the exposure of tests used in online research, researchers can control who sees their website. First, researchers can use password protection and control who receives the password. This is probably the most effective method of reducing test exposure. Many servers have built-in password protection, and free password protection systems are available on the Internet.

2.3.5 Avoiding harm

Social scientists must attempt to avoid and minimize harm to research participants. Many risks can be anticipated and minimized (e.g. confidentiality, invasion of privacy, drug treatment side effects). However, it is difficult to determine whether research has harmed participants in unexpected ways when researchers have no direct contact with the participants, as is usually the case in online research. If the researcher believes that there is a significant possibility of unintended harm in a particular study if little or no direct contact occurs, we recommend that the researcher increase the amount of contact or consider conducting the research in person. Some groups of people are more likely to be harmed than others, and additional steps should be used to protect their welfare.

Several ethical codes in the social sciences define the following as vulnerable populations: children, prisoners, pregnant women and people who are mentally disabled or economically or educationally disadvantaged. We recommend that studies involving these groups have higher levels of contact so that unintended harm can be prevented and detected. Researchers should provide multiple methods of contact (e.g. phone or address, as well as email) and should provide more information about potential risks. We also recommend that researchers pretest their study materials with people from the target population to determine whether modifications are necessary to avoid unintended harm.

2.4 Chapter summary

In this part of the book, we have presented and discussed the following topics:

- We explained the difference between obtrusive and unobtrusive methods and how it affects the ethical evaluation of our studies, in particular concerning the issue of informed consent. After, we discussed the role of informed consent in social scientific research using experiments. Digital data vary in terms of how much active the role of participants in the data collection process is. Obtrusive methods require participants' active engagement with a researcher's data collection. Unobtrusive methods can be conducted without the active participation of the people producing or eliciting data.

- Next, we have discussed the notions of minimal risk, deception and debriefing. The notion of minimal risk is particularly important here. Minimal risk is assessed when informed consent cannot be collected. Minimal risk is a condition in which participants involved in an experiment will be exposed to information or task that are not different from what they could encounter in their everyday life without causing them harm.

- We learned how to recognize the nature of data according to their privacy aspects. Concerning privacy, whenever full anonymization is not possible, recently the European GDPR has introduced the notion of pseudonymization, which is the processing of personal data in such a way that the data can no longer be attributed to a specific data subject without the use of additional information, as long as such additional information is kept separately and subject to technical and organizational measures to ensure non-attribution to an identified or identifiable individual.

- The last key point was understanding the approach of avoiding harm in social scientific research. Social scientists must attempt to avoid and minimize harm to research participants. Many risks can be anticipated and minimized (e.g. confidentiality, invasion of privacy, drug treatment side effects).

Further readings

While the ethics of digital social research is usually present in several methodological books, there are relatively few books exclusively dedicated to the ethics of digital research and none about the ethical aspects of online experiments. Nevertheless, useful texts that provide an overview of the main issues and debate around them are:

- the edited volume by Dobrick, Fischer and Hagen, *Research Ethics in the Digital Age: Ethics for the Social Sciences and Humanities in Times of Mediatization and Digitization* (2017);
- the edited book by Zimmer and Kinder-Kurlanda, *Internet Research Ethics for the Social Age: New Challenges, Cases and Contexts* (2017), that contains several case studies of ethical dilemmas in the context of online research, including experiments and conducting online in non-Western countries;
- the last book is Parsons' *Ethical Challenges in Digital Psychology and Cyberpsychology* (2019) that, while focussed on psychological research, contains many useful insights about online research, including online experiments. In addition, it is a text that deals with less mainstream yet digital methods: both the ethics of virtual reality research and video game used for social scientific studies.

3

CAUSAL INFERENCES AND EXPERIMENTS

━━━━━━━ Chapter objectives ━━━━━━━

- To introduce the notions of random assignment and average treatment effect
- To understand block random assignment
- To explain the move from full, factorial and optimal designs
- To explain the use of covariates in experiments' design

━━━━━━━ Key concepts ━━━━━━━

- A random assignment in experimental research has three important functions: (1) it distributes individual characteristics of participants across the treatment and control group so that they do not systematically affect the outcome of the experiment; (2) it helps ensure that error effects, which refer to the effect to the outcome variable not attributable to the manipulated variable, are statistically independent; and (3) it creates a group of respondents who are, at the time of such division, probabilistically similar on average.

(Continued)

- Block random assignment is a procedure whereby participants are partitioned into subgroups (called blocks or strata), and complete random assignment occurs within each block.
- Full factorial experiments are completely randomized designs, where *g* treatments are assigned at random to *N* units, and the treatments have had no structure; they were just *g* treatments.
- Factorial treatment structure exists when the *g* treatments are the combinations of the levels of two or more factors. We call these combination treatments factor-level combinations or factorial combinations to emphasize that each treatment is a combination of one level of each of the factors.
- Optimal design allocates treatments to units in such a way as to optimize some criteria; for example, we may wish to minimize the average variance of the estimated treatment effects. Optimal designs are created using search routines that depend on an optimality criterion.

3.1 Random assignment and average treatment effect

One crucial concept in experimental design is the notion of *random assignment* (Montgomery, 2009). A random assignment in experimental research has three important functions: (1) it distributes individual characteristics of participants across the treatment and control group so that they do not systematically affect the outcome of the experiment; (2) it helps ensure that error effects, which refer to the effect to the outcome variable not attributable to the manipulated variable, are statistically independent; and (3) it creates a group of respondents who are, at the time of such division, probabilistically similar on average. If the research has all the features of an experiment except random assignment, it is called a *quasi-experiment*. Unfortunately, the interpretation of quasi-experiments is often ambiguous. In the absence of random assignment, it is difficult to rule out all variables other than the independent variable as explanations for an observed result. Moreover, quasi-experiments may not have a control group, which therefore further complicates their validity.

The logic underlying randomized experiments is often explained in terms of a notational system that has its origins in Neyman (1923) and Rubin (1974) and that we present here in a summarized and simplified version. The formalized notation is as follows:

We have observation on N units indexed by $I = 1, \ldots, N$.

We use the binary indicator D_i to indicate whether the unit i was treated or not treated as a dummy variable with $D_{i=0}$ if unit i is not 'treated' (not shown the pop-up) and $D_{i=1}$ if unit i is treated (was shown the pop-up).

Y_i is the observed outcome (provided or not personal information) for each population unit i.

$Y_i = Y_{1i}$ if $D_i = 1$(unit i is treated)

$Y_i = Y_{1i}$ if $D_i = 0$(unit i is not treated)

Let $(Y_1, Y_0)_i$ be the two outcomes corresponding to the i-th population unit being treated or not treated, respectively

$Y_{1i} - Y_{0i}$ = unit level causal effect

Y_{0i} = the counterfactual for an individual who was shown the pop-up

Y_{1i} = the counterfactual for an individual who was not shown the pop-up

If a specific member of the population is exposed to the intervention, then Y_1 is observable, while Y_0 is irreversibly unobservable on that specific member. It follows that Y_1 and Y_0 are the factual and observable outcomes for treated and nontreated, respectively. The counterfactual outcome for a member of the population who was treated is Y_0 and for one who was not treated is Y_1. Henceforth, we simplify the notation by abandoning the index i and simply using the suffix 1 or 0, but with the important observation that blue refers to factual outcomes and red to counterfactual ones, as shown in Table 3.1.

Table 3.1 Factual and counterfactual outcomes

	Factual outcome	Counterfactual outcome
Treated ($D = 1$)	Y_1	Y_0
Nontreated ($D = 0$)	Y_0	Y_1

Now let us proceed by illustrating the standard logic identity focussing on the average treatment effect (ATE) on the treated.[1]

$$\text{Average Treatment on the Treated (ATT)} = E\{Y_1 - Y_0 | D = 1\}$$
$$= E\{Y_1 | D = 1\} - E\{Y_0 | D = 1\}$$

Evidently, the second term of the identity is unknown and unobservable as it represents the counterfactual for the treated; it means what a hypothetical subject who saw the pop-up would have done so had he or she not been shown the pop-up. Even more concretely, if we have Marc being shown the pop-up and deciding not to provide personal information, then the second term asks what Marc would have done had he not been shown the pop-up. Would he have provided the personal information or not?

Let us now consider the term $E\{(Y_1 | D = 1) - E\{Y_0 | D = 0\}$, which represents the factually observed difference in means between treated and nontreated, that is, observed and known; then we add and subtract to it the term $E\{Y_0 | D = 1\}$, which is the counterfactual for the nontreated. (Laura was not shown the pop-up. What would she have done had she been shown it? Again, this is unknown and unobservable.)

We, thus, get: **$E\{(Y_1 | D = 1) - E\{Y_0 | D = 0\} = [E\{Y_1 | D = 1\} - E$** __{$Y_0$ | $D = 1$}]__ + *[{E {Y_0 | $D = 1$} − E {Y_0 | $D = 0$}]*; in word (following the notation of using **bold**, underline and *italic*), this means that

---

[1]This is the causal effect of major interest from a policy perspective; the other important effect is the average treatment effect (ATE) defined as $E\{Y_1 - Y_0\}$ or the average effect that would result from having all population members (or none) take part in the programme. ATE perhaps is not a crucial parameter of interest for impact evaluation. It is the most relevant parameter when the programme under consideration is universal, in the sense that it would expose all units of the target population to treatment.

Observed Means Differences = Average Treatment on the Treated (ATT) + *Selection Bias*. So, the ATT and the selection bias cannot be disentangled, and simply calculating the difference in observed means will not suffice to identify the causal effect of the treatment on the treated. The selection bias term of the identity, $[\{E\{Y_0 \mid D = 1\} - E\{Y_0 \mid D = 0\}]$, can be easily interpreted as the difference in the outcome Y that would be observed between treated and non-treated if there was no treatment and depends on pre-existing differences between the two groups. That is, this term captures outcome differences between the treated and nontreated that cannot be attributed to the treatment. The first term of the selection bias is not observable. So, unless the selection bias is equal to zero or we can in some way control it (i.e. measure it), the full identity illustrated above cannot be given a causal interpretation. The selection bias is a function of X characteristics (possibly unobserved) of the treated and nontreated participants. In other words, we are saying that a vector of Xs variables shapes the values of the variable D or how the groups $D = 0$ and $D = 1$ are formed. Using some additional equations, which we will not replicate here, we can show that X is correlated to Y and hence the selection bias does not vanish, since the two groups (treated and nontreated) are not equivalent with regard to Xs. In other words, there is a selection bias when (1) being treated or not depends on individual characteristics X known to affect also the outcome variable and (2) such characteristics are unequally distributed between the treated and the nontreated.

Under the condition of a randomized experiment, the selection bias vanishes and then we can basically recover the causal effect as a simple difference in means. Under randomization, the dummy variable D depends on the toss of a coin and is not systematically related to either Y or Xs in anyway; hence, the selection bias of the previous identity entirely vanishes (equal to zero). In effect, if we randomize participants either to be exposed to a pop-up or not, their unobserved characteristics would no longer be related to how they browse a website and the related changes of coming or not across the pop-up. Well-performed randomization ensures that the treated and nontreated groups are balanced with respect to these unobserved characteristics.

Under the condition of randomization, then, the treatment effect is estimated as a difference between two means. Statistically, such a difference in mean can be obtained (if it exists) by running a regression analysis where the dependent variable is our outcome Y (in the exemplification, we used the provision of personal information) and the independent variable is a dummy equal to one if the subject has seen the pop-up and zero otherwise. Let 'y' be, for instance, 'provision of personal information' measured with respect to whether participants saw a pop-up ($D = 1$) or not ($D = 0$). Hence, the general formula for the y is

$$y = a + b D_1 + \epsilon$$

The term ϵ includes all the observable and unobservable variables that impact on Y. What is important is that under randomization, the expected value of ϵ under treatment (in technical notation $E[\epsilon \mid D_1]$) is equal to zero (orthogonality condition). A simple ordinary least square (OLS) regression is capable of identifying 'b', since the exogeneity condition is met. The coefficient 'b' is precisely the treatment effect. In fact, for those that did not receive the treatment, the expected value for y is

$$E[y|D_1 = 0] = y_0 = a$$

while for the treated group, we have

$$E[y|D_1 = 1] = y_1 = a + b$$

So, by definition:

$$b = y_1 - y_0$$

This corresponds to the difference in the mean outcome between treated and untreated group, that is, the treatment effect. The coefficient 'b' is also what we can consistently estimate with OLS.

3.2 Block random assignment

Block random assignment is a procedure whereby participants are partitioned into subgroups (called blocks or strata), and complete random assignment occurs within each block. For example, suppose we have 20 participants in our experiment, 10 men and 10 women. Suppose our experimental design calls for 10 participants to be placed into the treatment condition. If we were to use complete random assignment, chances are that we would end up with unequal numbers of men and women in the treatment group. However, block randomization ensures equal numbers of men and women will be assigned to each experimental condition. First, we partition the subject pool into men and women. We randomly assign five into the treatment group; from the pool of female participants, we randomly assign five into the treatment group. In effect, block randomization creates a series of miniature experiments, one per block.

Block randomized designs are used to address a variety of practical and statistical concerns. Sometimes programme requirements dictate how many participants of each type to place in the treatment group. Imagine, for example, that a summer reading programme aimed at elementary school students seeks to evaluate its impact on school performance and retention during the following academic year. The school can admit only a small fraction of those who apply, and school administrators worry that if too many children with low levels of preparedness are admitted to the programme, teachers will find it challenging to manage their classes effectively. Therefore, these administrators insist that 60% of the children admitted to the pro-gramme pass an initial test of basic skills. The way to address this concern is by blocking on initial test scores and allocating students within each block so that 60% of the students who are randomly admitted to the programme have passed the basic skills test. For example, imagine that the school can admit 50 of the 100 applicants. Forty of the applicants failed the initial examination, and 60 passed. Thus, the researcher could create two blocks: one block of students who passed the basic skills test and another block of students who failed. Each block is sorted in random order, and the researcher selects the first 20 students in the block containing those who failed the basic skills test and the first 30 students in the block containing students who passed the test. This procedure ensures that the 60% requirement is satisfied. This design approach comes in handy when resource constraints prevent researchers from treating more than a certain number of participants from certain regions or when concerns about fairness dictate that treatments be apportioned equally across demographic groups.

Block randomization also addresses two important statistical concerns. First, blocking helps reduce sampling variability. Sometimes the researcher is able to partition the participants into blocks such that the participants in each block have similar potential outcomes. For example, students who fail the basic skills test presumably share similar potential outcomes; the same goes for students who pass the basic skills test. By randomizing within each block, the researcher eliminates the possibility of rogue randomizations that, by chance, place all of the students who fail the basic skills test into the treatment group. Under simple or complete random assignment, these outlandish assignments rarely occur; under block random assignment, they are ruled out entirely. Second, blocking ensures that specific subgroups are available for separate analysis.

When designing, a block randomization is useful in calculating the number of possible assignments under complete random assignment and the blocked random assignment. Let $0 < m < N$. Of N observations, m are placed into the treatment group, and $N - m$ are placed into the control group. The number of possible randomizations under complete random assignment is

$$\frac{N!}{m!(N - m)!} \tag{3.1}$$

For example, the number of randomizations under complete random assignment when $N = 20$ and $m = 10$ is

$$\frac{20!}{10!10!} = 184,756$$

To calculate the number of possible random assignments under a blocked design with B blocks, calculate the number of random allocations in each block: $r_1, r_2, \ldots, r_B$. The total number of random assignments is $r_1 X, r_2 X, \ldots, X r_B$. For example, when we randomly assign half of the 10 men to treatment and half of the 10 women to treatment, there are

$$\left(\frac{10!}{5!5!}\right)\left(\frac{10!}{5!5!}\right) = 63,504$$

The next step is to calculate the standard error in a blocked design. The formula for any number of blocks is

$$SE\left(\widehat{ATE}\right) = \sqrt{\sum_1^j \left(\frac{N_j}{N}\right)^2 SE^2\left(\widehat{ATE}_j\right)} \tag{3.2}$$

Hence, for example, for a two-block design, the standard error to assess the uncertainty of both groups combined is

$$SE\left(\widehat{ATE}\right) = \sqrt{(SE_1)^2\left(\frac{N_1}{N}\right)^2 + (SE_2)^2\left(\frac{N_2}{N}\right)^2} \tag{3.3}$$

Notice that to calculate $SE(\widehat{ATE}_j)$ for each block, every block must contain at least two observations in treatment and two observations in control. This requirement will not be met by *matched pair designs*, experiments in which every block contains just two participants, one of which is assigned to treatment. Fortunately, analysis of matched pair experiments is straightforward. The ATE is estimated by subtracting the control outcome from the treatment outcome in each block and averaging over all blocks. (Because the probability of assignment to the treatment group is 0.5 for all blocks, one obtains identical estimates by subtracting the average outcome among the $N/2$ participants in the control condition from the average outcome among the $N/2$ participants in the treatment condition.) These block-level differences are then used to estimate the standard error:

$$\widehat{SE}\left(\widehat{ATE}\right) = \sqrt{\frac{1}{\frac{N}{2}\left(\frac{N}{2}-1\right)}\sum_{j=1}^j \left(\widehat{ATE}_j - \widehat{ATE}\right)^2} \sqrt{\frac{1}{J(J-1)}\sum_{j=1}^j \left(\widehat{ATE}_j - \widehat{ATE}\right)^2} \tag{3.4}$$

To calculate the standard error, we first calculate the standard error for the matched pair part of the experiment using this equation and then combine the standard error for the matched pair part of the design with the standard errors from the other block using Eq. (3.3).

Blocking provides a way to address two classes of design objectives. The first arises when practical or ethical imperatives dictate the number of treatments that may be assigned to certain groups of participants. Blocking allows the researcher to build a randomized experiment around these constraints. The second set of objectives has to do with statistical precision. When grouping participants with similar potential outcomes forms blocks, substantial improvements in precision are possible, particularly in small samples. Does blocking have a downside? Although it is possible to construct perverse examples in which blocking harms precision, blocking rarely has negative consequences in practice. Even blocking participants into random subsets (which does nothing to group participants according to their potential outcomes) is an experimental design that is no worse, in terms of the precision with which the ATE is calculated, than complete random assignment. In practice, the biggest downside associated with blocking is the risk that the data will be misanalyzed. The ATE must be estimated block by block when the probability of treatment assignment varies by block, and care must be taken to conduct hypothesis tests in a manner that follows the exact procedure by which the randomization was carried out.

Sometimes block randomization is not feasible. It is not uncommon for field experiments to be conducted under severe time constraints, and background information necessary to form blocks may be unavailable at the time of random allocation. Similarly, the implementation of randomization within blocks may exceed the technical capacity of those implementing random allocation in field settings. Nevertheless, failure to block randomize should not be regarded as a serious design flaw, especially in studies where the treatment and control groups contain more than 100 participants.

3.3 Basic experiments' layouts

If you are a researcher who 'follows the old standard *rule of one variable*, [holding] all the conditions constant except for one factor which is his *experimental factor* or his *independent variable*' and he or she has no compelling reasons to engage in local control of classificatory factors, the randomization plan consists in assigning at chance the t treatment levels to the N available experimental units (or, which is the same, assigning at the chance the N experimental units to the t treatment levels). The resulting design is called *completely randomized design*, and the randomization procedure is known as sequential random assignment (SRA). This is the foundation on which we build more complex experimental designs. SRA refers to equal probabilities of assignment. In other words, each experimental unit has an equal probability of being assigned to each of the treatment levels included in the design. To carry out SRA, we begin by associating, term by term, a series of random numbers to the entries of an allocation frame. Units in the allocation frame must be unambiguously identified and sequentially numerated $(1 - n)$.

With a small number of experimental units (or participants), such design often does not produce a balanced design because some treatment levels' groups turn out to be constituted by different set participants compared to other groups. Therefore, if we have a small number of participants, we aim to achieve a balanced design introducing some constraints. This way, we can obtain a good trade-off between resources and the statistical power of our experiments. We can, therefore, use a 'Forced Equal Sizes' approach to ensure that all experimental conditions have the same number of experimental units. The same logic can be applied in terms of experimental units/participants stratification. We want to make sure that all experimental groups have enough individuals with all the characteristics that might play a role in their performance, for example, age and education.

In some specific cases, we want to use the opposite approach. In other words, we might have theoretical or practical reasons for specific comparisons which need more statistical power compared to less important ones. In this case, we can use a 'Forced Unequal Sizes' design. Last, there is the possibility of using unequal probabilities of assignment as a feature in the context of adaptive randomization procedures that will be discussed later.

In classic randomized experiments based on between-subject design, a subject is typically allocated to only one experimental condition: either to one treatment or to one control group. This is the best approach when the conditions to be tested are few and the design very simple. With many conditions to be tested and a complex design, the solution is a between-participants design with partial repetition of measures or a full-blown within-participants design; in the first instance, participants can be exposed to more than one experimental condition, and in the second instance, all participants are used with every condition tested in the experiment, including the control one. The main advantage is that using the same participants for many conditions is, in practice, like increasing statistical power. Put it the other way around and recalling our earlier discussion about statistical power and minimum detectable effect, whereas with 120 participants we can test a maximum of three treatments and one control in a between-participants design, this can be multiplied by some factors (but not too much, otherwise undesired effects kick in too heavily) if each subject is used in more than one condition. Within-participants design presents several challenges that are not present in between-subject design: order effects, learning effects, hypothesis guessing and fatigue. All these effects, if not balanced, introduce noise and threaten construct validity.

Imagine a situation where all participants go through treatment A, B and C in this exact order. Three outcomes are possible: (1) going through A before B may influence the reaction to B, which means we can no longer assume that the effect of B on the response variable X is due just to B; (2) when participants arrive at C, they may be tired and their reactions will reflect their mental state more than the effect of treatment C; and (3) it is possible that going through A, B and C in this order enables the participants to understand what the researcher is trying to prove. They can, thus, engage in hypothesis guessing and answer either way so to please the researchers or to refute his or her hypothesis. In all three cases, construct validity is weakened, and the causal effect measured may be the result of biases rather than of the treatments.

3.4 Full, factorial and optimal designs

We have been working with completely randomized designs, where g treatments are assigned at random to N units. Up till now, the treatments have had no structure; they were just g treatments. Factorial treatment structure exists when the g treatments are the combinations of the levels of two or more factors. We call these combination treatments factor-level combinations or factorial combinations to emphasize that each treatment is a combination of one level of each of the factors. We have not changed the randomization; we still have a completely randomized design. It is just that now we are considering treatments that have a factorial structure.

There are many experimental designs possible, but basic types are those that focus on one independent variable (or manipulated variable), called 'single-factor' experiments, and those that study the role of multiple independent variables, or 'multi-factor' experiments. The latter can have several levels assumed by the independent variables. For example, a 2×2 multiple factor design is a study that refers to the structure of an experiment that studies the effects of a pair of two-level independent variables. The independent variables are manipulated to create four different sets of conditions, and the researcher measures the effects of the independent variables on the dependent variable.

The advantage of factorial designs can be easily illustrated. Suppose we have two factors, A and B, each at two levels (Figure 3.1 – top). If we denote the levels of the factors by $A-$, $A+$, $B-$ and $B+$, the effect of changing factor A is given by $A+B- - A-B-$, and the effect of changing factor B is given by $A-B+ - A-B-$. Because experimental error is present, it is desirable to take two observations, say, at each treatment combination and estimate the effects of the factors using average responses. Thus, a total of six observations are required. If a factorial experiment had been performed, an additional treatment combination, $A+B+$, would have been taken. Now, using

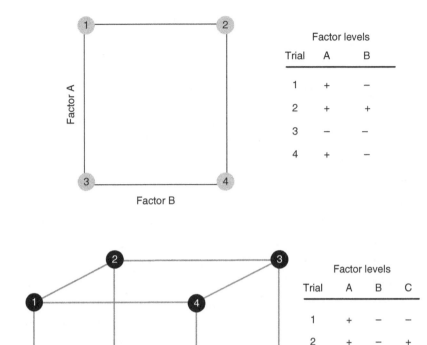

Figure 3.1 Factorial structures in experiments

just *four* observations, two estimates of the A effect can be made: $A+B- - A-B-$ and $A+B+ - A-B+$. Similarly, two estimates of the B effect can be made. These two estimates of each main effect could be averaged to produce average main effects that are *just as precise* as those from the single-factor experiment, but only four total observations are required, and we would say that the relative efficiency of the factorial design to the one-factor-at-a-time experiment is $(6/4) = 1.5$. Now suppose interaction is present. If the one-factor-at-a-time design indicated that $A-B+$ and $A+B-$ gave better responses than $A-B-$, a logical conclusion would be that $A+B+$

would be even better. However, if interaction is present, this conclusion may be seriously in error.

Factorial designs have several advantages and are more efficient than one-factor-at-a-time experiments. Furthermore, a factorial design is necessary in cases where interactions may be present that might result in misleading conclusions. Finally, factorial designs allow the effects of a factor to be estimated at several levels of the other factors, yielding conclusions that are valid over a range of experimental conditions. Factorial design can be complicated by the introduction of blocking and counterbalancing. The latter is when people work through the conditions in different orders; it distributes order effects evenly over the conditions being compared.

Factorial designs allow researchers to study the way in which the treatment effect of one variable changes depending on the levels of other randomly assigned factors. When the number of factors and conditions is large, it may be impractical to assign participants to every combination of conditions. Designs that omit some combinations are termed 'fractional' factorial designs. The design of fractional factorial experiments is itself the subject of entire reference texts.

Factorial treatment structure has two advantages:

- When the factors interact, factorial experiments can estimate the interaction. One-at-at-time experiments cannot estimate interaction. Use of one-at-a-time experiments in the presence of interaction can lead to serious misunderstanding of how the response varies as a function of the factors.
- When the factors do not interact, factorial experiments are more efficient than one-at-a-time experiments, in that the units can be used to assess the (main) effects for both factors. Units in a one-at-a-time experiment can only be used to assess the effects of one factor.

There are thus two times when you should use factorial treatment structure when your factors interact, and when your factors do not interact. Factorial structure is a win, whether or not we have interaction.

3.4.1 Optimal designs

The final possibility that we mention is that we can have blocks with different numbers of units; that is, some blocks have more units than others. Standard designs assume that all blocks have the same number of units, so we must do something special. The most promising approach is probably optimal design via special design software. Optimal design allocates treatments to units in such a way as to optimize some criteria; for example, we may wish to minimize the average variance of the estimated treatment effects. Optimal designs are created using search routines that depend on an optimality criterion. The most common optimality criteria are

- 'D-optimality'
- 'Bayesian D-optimality'
- 'I-optimality'
- 'Bayesian I-optimality'
- 'A-optimality'
- 'Alias optimality'

In the context of this book, the criteria of particular interest are the D, I and A. First, we will discuss the **D-optimality** as it is common in the use of screening design, a form of optimal design increasingly common in online experiments.

The D-optimality criterion minimizes the determinant of the covariance matrix of the model coefficient estimates. It follows that D-optimality focusses on precise estimates of the effects. This criterion is desirable in the following cases:

- Screening designs
- Experiments that focus on estimating effects or testing for significance
- Designs where identifying the active factors is the experimental goal

The D-optimality criterion is dependent on the assumed model. This is a limitation because often the form of the true model is not known in advance. The runs of a D-optimal design optimize the precision of the coefficients of the assumed model. In the extreme, a D-optimal design might be saturated, with the same number of runs as parameters and no degrees of freedom for lack of fit.

Specifically, a D-optimal design maximizes D, where D is defined as follows:

$$D = \det[X'X] \tag{3.5}$$

where X is the model matrix. D-optimal split designs maximize D, where D is defined as follows:

$$D = \det[X'V^{-1}X] \tag{3.6}$$

where V^{-1} is the block diagonal covariance matrix of the responses (Goos, 2002).

There is also the Bayesian D-optimality, which is a modification of the D-optimality criterion. The Bayesian D-optimality criterion is useful when there are potentially active interactions or non-linear effects (see DuMouchel & Jones, 1994; Jones et al., 2008).

The second criterion to consider is I-optimality. I-optimal designs minimize the average variance of prediction over the design space. The I-optimality criterion is more appropriate than D-optimality if your primary experimental goal is not to estimate coefficients, but rather to do the following:

- Predict a response
- Determine optimum operating conditions
- Determine regions in the design space where the response falls within an acceptable range

In these cases, precise prediction of the response takes precedence over precise estimation of the parameters. The prediction variance relative to the unknown error variance at a point X_0 in the design space can be calculated as follows:

$$\mathrm{var}\left(\widehat{Y}|X_o\right) = f(X_0)'(X'X)^{-1}f(X_0) \tag{3.7}$$

where X is the model matrix. I-optimal designs minimize the integral I of the prediction variance over the entire design space, where I is given as follows:

$$I = \int_R f(x')(X'X)^{-1}f(x)dx = \text{trace}\left[(X'X)^{-1}M\right] \tag{3.8}$$

Here M is the moments matrix:

$$M = \int_R f(x)f(x)' dx \tag{3.9}$$

The moments matrix does not depend on the design and can be computed in advance. The row vector $f(\mathbf{x})'$ consists of a 1 followed by the effects corresponding to the assumed model. For example, for a full quadratic model in two continuous factors, $f(\mathbf{x})'$ is defined as follows:

$$f(x)' = \left(1,\ x_1, x_2, x_1x_2, x_1^2, x_2^2\right) \tag{3.10}$$

Use an **A-optimal design** when you want to put emphasis on certain model effects. An A-optimal design enables you to assign weights to your model parameters. These weights are used in the A-optimality criterion to select the design. The resulting design will place more emphasis on factor combinations that lower the variance of the estimates for highly weighted terms than for terms with lower weights. For example, you may have a group of interactions that are more important to estimate than other interactions. You can increase the weights on the key interactions to decrease the variance of their estimates as compared to the other interactions. The A-optimality criterion minimizes the trace of the covariance matrix of the model coefficient estimates. The trace is the sum of the main diagonal elements of a matrix. An A-optimal design minimizes the sum of the variances of the regression coefficients.

Screening designs are quite popular in online experiments. Typically used in the initial stages of experimentation, they examine many factors to identify those factors that have the greatest effect on the response. The factors that are identified are then studied using more sensitive designs. Because screening designs generally require fewer experimental runs than other designs, they are a relatively inexpensive and efficient way to begin improving a process. If a standard screening design exists for your experimental situation, you can choose from several standard screening designs. The list includes blocked designs when applicable. Your factors can be two-level continuous factors, three-level categorical factors or continuous factors that can assume only discrete values (discrete numeric factors). However, there are situations where standard screening designs are not available. In these cases, researchers construct a main effects screening design. A main effects screening design is either orthogonal or near orthogonal. It focusses on estimating main effects in the presence of negligible interactions.

Screening experiments tend to be small and are aimed at identifying the factors that affect a response. Because identification is the goal (rather than sophisticated modelling), continuous factors in a screening design are typically set at only two levels. However, a screening situation might also involve discrete numeric or categorical factors, in which case classical screening designs might not fit your situation. The screening design can handle all three types of factors: two-level continuous factors, categorical factors and discrete numeric factors. There are two types of designs:

- Classical designs: For situations where standard screening designs exist, you can choose from a list that includes fractional factorial designs, Plackett–Burman, Cotter and mixed-level designs.
- Main effects screening designs: Whether a standard design is available, you can construct a main effects screening design. These designs are orthogonal or near orthogonal and focus on estimating main effects in the presence of negligible interactions.

The emphasis on studying main effects early in the experimentation process is supported by the empirical principle of effect hierarchy. This principle maintains that lower-order effects are more likely to be important than higher-order effects. For this reason, screening designs focus on identifying active main effects. In cases where higher-order interactions are of interest, screening designs assume that two-factor interactions are more important than three-factor interactions and so on (see Hamada and Wu, 2009).

The efficiency of screening designs also depends on the principle of effect sparsity. The principle of effect sparsity asserts that most of the variation in the response is explained by a relatively small number of effects. Screening designs, where many effects are studied, rely heavily on effect sparsity. Experience shows that the number of runs used in a screening design should be at least twice the number of effects that are likely to be significant.

To appreciate the importance of effect sparsity, consider an example where you have seven two-level factors. Contrast a full factorial design to a screening design:

- A full factorial design consists of all combinations of the levels of the factors. The number of runs is the product of the numbers of levels for each factor. In this example, a full factorial design has $2^7 = 128$ runs.
- In contrast, a screening design requires only a fraction of the runs in the full factorial design. The main effects of the seven factors can be studied in an eight-run screening design.

3.5 Using covariates in experimental design and analysis

One attractive feature of randomized experiments is that they generate unbiased estimates of the ATE regardless of whether the researcher accounts for other causes of the outcome. The problem of *omitted variables* that torment nonexperimental research is addressed by random assignment. Randomly assigned treatments are statistically independent of all observed and unobserved variables. Any correlation between the treatment and other factors that affect outcomes arises purely by chance due to how observations happened to be allocated to treatment and control groups. Because the 7 controls the assignment process, the sampling distribution of estimated ATEs can be studied rigorously, and precise inferences may be drawn when evaluating the sharp null hypothesis of no treatment effect. Experimentation makes causal inference possible even when the researcher has a very limited understanding of why some observations have different potential outcomes than others.

Although *covariates*, or supplementary variables that predict outcomes, are not required for unbiased estimation, they may be put to good use when available. There are several useful roles that covariates play in experimental design and analysis. We begin by discussing three ways in which covariates may be used in the analysis of experimental data. One technique is to use covariates to rescale the dependent variable so that potential outcomes have minor variance, improving the precision with which treatment effects may be estimated. A second technique, regression analysis, uses covariates to eliminate observed differences between treatment and control groups and to reduce the variability in outcomes. The net effect is usually an improvement in the precision with which the treatment effect is estimated. Regression may also be used to check for data-handling errors that potentially undermine random assignment of observations to treatment and control groups. The third use of covariates is block randomized experimental design, which we introduced previously. The researcher forms a set of relatively homogenous groups or blocks based on intuitions about which covariates are likely to predict outcomes, each with different expected outcomes. Random assignment to treatment and control is conducted separately within each block.

Let us first discuss the use of regression to deal with differences in outcomes. An alternative to rescaling the outcome is to expand the regression model by including one or more covariates as right-hand-side predictors and an approach called *regression adjustment* or *covariate adjustment*. What was before a regression of Y on d now becomes a regression of Y_i on d_i and X_i. The regression model may be written as follows:

$$Y_i = Y_i(0)(1 - d_i) + Y_i(1)d_i = a + bd_i + cX_i + (u - cX_i) \qquad (3.11)$$

where the disturbance is the last term in parentheses, and if the regression estimate of c is close to 1, regression adjustment and rescaled regression will generate very similar estimates of b. A note of warning, it should be clear that the regression estimate c has no causal interpretation. The values of Y are unaffected by X; the middle part of Eq. (3.5) underscores this point by reiterating that Y is solely a function of potential outcomes and treatment status. X plays no role in the causal process – using an accounting identity, we added it to the regression model and subtracted it from the disturbance term. The only reason to include X as a regressor is that doing so subtracts cX from the disturbance. When X predicts outcomes, this subtraction reduces the amount of unexplained variation in Y, which in turn reduces the standard error of $\hat{b}$. In other words, the decision to include X in the regression model is based on whether it is thought to *predict* outcomes; we remain agnostic about whether X *affects* outcomes.

What is the advantage of using covariates as regressors? The answer is flexibility. We can include several covariates as right-hand-side variables and let OLS determine their respective scaling parameters. In principle, this approach reduces disturbance variability more effectively than rescaled regression, enabling us to estimate b more precisely.

Are there drawbacks to using regression to control for covariates? In small samples ($N < 20$), controlling for covariates can lead to bias, and rescaling the outcome is probably a safer strategy than regression adjustment. However, in larger samples ($N > 20$), the inclusion of a single covariate typically leads to negligible bias. To avoid bias, regression models that include multiple covariates should have at least 20 more observations than covariates. Whether the inclusion of covariates leads to a reduction in standard error depends on the application.

Another application of the use of covariate is to use them to detect administrative errors in the implementation of the assignments in experimental conditions. The random assignment of any finite number of observations inevitably produces some degree of *imbalance* or correlation between the assigned treatment and one or more covariates. By controlling for covariates, whether through rescaling the dependent variable or through regression adjustment, the researcher re-establishes balance.

For example, if one estimates a regression like Eq. (3.5), the regression will eliminate any linear relationship between the assigned treatment and the pre-test. If one wanted to eliminate both linear and non-linear relationships between the treatment and the covariate while allowing for possibly non-linear relationships between the covariate and the outcome, one could either control for a polynomial function of the pre-test (such as X, X_2 and X_3) or code the pre-test as a series of indicator variables in order to examine treatment effects among those who share the same pre-test score. The broader point is that imbalance on measured indicators is a tractable problem that can be handled by methods such as regression analysis.

Imbalance is a cause for concern not because it presents an insurmountable estimation problem, but because it may call into question the soundness of the random assignment procedure or the administrative handling of the data. When concerns like these arise, the first thing to do is retrace the steps that were taken when the observations were randomly assigned. Does the dataset contain the random numbers on which the random assignment was based? If so, do the treatment assignments appear to follow the randomly speci- fied schedule? Is there a computer program that reproduces the random numbers and the process by which they were used to guide the allocation of participants? These kinds of internal audits may solve the mystery by reference to the randomization procedure itself or other administrative problems that caused some observations to be excluded, double-counted or miscoded.

One way to bolster confidence in the integrity of the randomization procedure and the administrative care with which the data were handled is to provide a statistical description of the balance between treatment and control groups on a range of available covariates. Often, one of the first tables in a research article reports the distri- bution of pre-test scores and other covariates for each of the experimental groups. This table enables the reader to assess two things. First, do prognostic variables, such as pre-test scores, differ appreciably between treatment and control groups? If so, this pattern will help the reader understand why the estimated ATE varies depending on whether covariates are included. Second, for the entire set of covariates, are the imbalances larger than one would expect from chance alone? This question can be answered by means of a statistical test and accompanying simulation. For binary treatments, the statistical test involves a regression of the assigned treatment on all of the covariates and calculation of the F-statistic. Alternatively, one may use logistic regression and calculate the log-likelihood statistic. For experiments with many treatments, the same regression is performed using multinomial logistic regression, and again one calculates a log-likelihood statistic.

Does random imbalance on measured covariates mean that the experimental estimates are biased? Bias is a property of an estimation procedure, not a specific estimate. The randomly assigning observations to treatment and control generate unbiased estimates of the ATE, even though some estimates are too high or too low, and some samples display covariate imbalance. Ex-ante (i.e. before we conduct our random assignment), we expect our experimental procedure to render the ATE on average.

The bottom line is that if a covariate is imbalanced due to random assignment, controlling for this imbalance produces unbiased estimates. In practice, if you find evidence of imbalance in a continuous covariate, you may wish to control for this variable using a flexible functional form. For example, if you were to find imbalance on a pre-test score, you might want to control for the pre-test score as well as squared values of the pre-test score. Sometimes researchers worry that observed imbalance is symptomatic of a broader problem of imbalance among other unobserved factors that affect outcomes. So long as imbalance is solely due to random chance (as opposed to administrative error) and so long as we control for the covariate that is imbalanced, there is no reason to expect imbalance on other covariates or on unmeasured causes of the outcome variable.

By making smart use of covariates, experimental researchers can improve the precision with which ATEs are estimated. Sometimes the improvement is dramatic, equivalent to a marked increase in the number of observations. The challenge is to use covariates in a principled way because any gain in precision can be offset by procedures that potentially introduce bias. Thus, covariates should be chosen from the set of variables that exist before the random intervention. Ideally, the particular covariates that the researcher wishes to control should be specified before seeing the experimental outcomes; otherwise, the selective use of covariates raises concerns about whether the researcher is trying to guide the estimates towards a particular result. Block randomized designs are particularly appealing in this regard. Although blocking often produces a relatively small gain in precision over after-the-fact regression adjustment of entirely randomized experiments, blocking has the virtue of embodying ex-ante expectations about prognostic variables and a specific model for estimating treatment effects. If the probability of treatment assignment varies by block, be sure to take this aspect of the design into account when analyzing the data; comparing unweighted outcomes in treatment and control groups may produce severely biased estimates if treatment probabilities are correlated with potential outcomes.

Covariates are of particular value to researchers who must conduct experiments under severe budget constraints. Squeezing every drop of precision out of an experiment requires a bit of extra effort and ingenuity. Therefore, researchers should be on the lookout for target populations for which extensive background information is readily available. The Swedish government, for example, makes available to researchers extraordinarily detailed information about its citizens' school records, employment history and health records. Researchers conducting surveys or social network mapping may have rich data on individuals who could later be the participants of an experimental intervention. Firms that distribute credit or discount cards sometimes have extensive information about the purchasing behaviour of their customers. Experiments that are built on these databases start with a wealth of prognostic covariates.

Covariates also assist in the detection of administrative errors. Mistakes are inevitable in collecting and processing primary data, and one virtue of random assignment is that it creates well-defined statistical patterns that can be detected with the aid of covariates. Of course, no error detection method is foolproof, but when covariates are strongly related to treatment assignment, researchers should review the procedures used to allocate observations to experimental groups.

One danger in mixing covariates into the analysis of experimental data is the temptation to interpret covariates in causal terms. It is not uncommon to encounter research articles in which authors offer a causal interpretation for all the regression coefficients they present, including the coefficients associated with pre-test scores, blocking indicators and other factors that are not subject to random assignment.

Attaching a causal story to these coefficients is at odds with the experimental approach, which uses random assignment to build a stock of defensible causal claims. The coefficients associated with covariates are uninterpretable without solid substantive assumptions. The set of covariates included in an experimental analysis need not be a complete list of factors that affect outcomes; some factors that are left out or are poorly measured are not a source of bias when the aim is to measure the ATE of the random intervention. However, omission and mismeasurement can lead to severe bias if the aim is to draw causal inferences about the effects of covariates. Causal interpretation of the covariates encounters all threats to inference associated with the analysis of observational data.

3.6 Chapter summary

In this chapter, we have discussed the foundational blocks of experimental design, discussing the following topics:

- We have introduced the notions of random assignment and ATE. A random assignment in experimental research has three important functions: (1) it distributes individual characteristics of participants across the treatment and control group so that they do not systematically affect the outcome of the experiment it helps ensure that error effects, which refer to the effect to the outcome variable not attributable to the manipulated variable, are statistically independent; and (2) it creates a group of respondents who are, at the time of such division, probabilistically similar on average.

- Next, we have discussed the role of block random assignment in experimental design. Block random assignment is a procedure whereby participants are partitioned into subgroups (called blocks or strata), and complete random assignment occurs within each block.

- With these two notions, we were able to discuss the fundamentals of experimental design in terms of full, factorial and optimal designs. Full factorial experiments are completely randomized designs, where g treatments are assigned at random to N units, and the treatments have had no structure; they were just g treatments. Factorial treatment structure exists when the g treatments are the combinations of the levels of two or more factors. We call these combination treatments factor-level combinations or factorial combinations to emphasize that each treatment is a combination of one level of each of the factors. Last, we discussed optimal designs. An optimal design allocates treatments to units in such a way as to optimize some criteria; for example, we may wish to minimize the average variance of the estimated treatment effects. Optimal designs are created using search routines that depend on an optimality criterion.

- The last issue that we have discussed is the use of covariates in experiments' design. There are several useful roles that covariates play in experimental design and analysis. We presented the three ways in which covariates may be used in the analysis of experimental data.

Further readings

There are a lot of texts available about experimental design, but surprisingly few that are specific to web experiments. There is one classic edited text that is always useful, even though it is now rather outdated concerning the Internet and the WWW, especially in the aftermath of the Web 2.0 revolution: Birnbaum's (2009) *Psychological Experiments on the Internet*. No other books are available specific to web experiments.

Moving to more general issues of design, excellent reference books are: Alferes's (2012) *Methods of Randomization in Experimental Design* and Lawson's (2015) *Design and Analysis of Experiments with R*. In addition, an excellent book concerning randomized controlled trials is Solomon et al.'s (2009) *Randomized Controlled Trials: Design and Implementation for Community-Based Psychosocial Interventions*. Also, Dunning's *Natural Experiments in the Social Sciences* (2012) contains many valid insights even though it deals with other 'family of experiments'.

4

SAMPLING FOR POPULATION-BASED SURVEY EXPERIMENTS

━━━━━ Chapter objectives ━━━━━

- To describe the various forms of sampling that are employed in online experiments, in particular in population-based survey experiments (PBSEs)
- To introduce the role of adaptive design
- To discuss the role of attrition in online experiments

━━━━━ Key concepts ━━━━━

- There are five different types of probability sample-based web surveys: (1) Intercept surveys. This type is the online equivalent of offline surveys based on systematic sampling, which is the selection of every k^{th} element from a sampling frame or from a sequential stream of potential respondents. (2) List-based samples. In this case, the sample is recruited from a list of people who form a well-defined population. (3) Mixed-mode surveys with Internet-based option.

(Continued)

Traditional surveys can be combined with a web option, in which case a web survey is available to respondents of a traditionally selected probability sample. (4) Pre-recruited online panels of Internet users. In this category are web surveys that use a panel made up of a probability sample of Internet users. (5) Pre-recruited online panels of the population. This is the most expensive, but also the most complete option. A representative sample of the population is constructed using traditional sampling criteria (e.g. tax records as sampling frame) and Internet access is given access to those who do not have it, thereby allowing them to respond to web surveys.

- The general objective in adaptive survey design (ASD) is to tailor the protocol to sample members in order to improve targeted survey outcomes. The basic premise of adaptive interventions is shared by ASDs – tailoring methods to individuals based on interim outcomes. We label these dynamic adaptive designs to reflect the dynamic nature of the optimization and static adaptive designs when they are based solely on information available prior to the start of data collection.

- Attrition occurs when outcome data are missing. Certain forms of attrition pose a grave threat to unbiased inference. When attrition is systematically related to potential outcomes, removing observations from the dataset means that remaining subjects assigned to the treatment or control group no longer constitute random samples of the original collection of participants, and therefore a comparison of group averages may no longer be an unbiased estimator of the average treatment effect.

4.1 From subject pools to samples

We have discussed issues of accuracy while discussing the design issues related to the development of online experiments. We now focus on the issue of coverage error, which is the most common source of concern using this methodology. In general, we can distinguish between, as in the case of web surveys, non-probability sample-based web surveys and those that use a probability sample.

Among the non-probability samples web surveys, there are three broad types:

1. Web polls for instant response. These are polls conducted online by web news sites; there is no claim of representativeness and participants coincide with the visitors of the webpage hosting the poll.
2. Unrestricted self-selected web surveys. This type refers to web surveys that use open invitation to recruit participants on web pages, social media, etc. Again, there is no representativeness involved and participants are recruited by self-selection (no selection criteria from researchers). Graduate students start learning how to design web surveys using this type.
3. Volunteer-based (opt-in) panels. In this case, respondents are chosen from lists of people recruited online by means of open invitation. The so-called 'web panels' are not curated to have representativeness, participation and performance are not incentivized and participants are self-selected.

While the first two cases are not usually included in social scientific research, the third is a different story. Self-selected volunteer panels have their scientific uses, and much depends on the nature of the study and the assumed transportability of the (potential) findings. As discussed previously, this concerns the issue of 'transportability' of pattern found in one subset of a population to other parts of it or other populations (Pearl and Bareinboim, 2014). Whether such panels can be used to represent any larger population is open to question. In some cases, the results are intended to be projected onto the general population, and sophisticated weighting procedures are used to reduce the coverage and non-response biases associated with the use of self-selected panellists for this purpose.

Moving to examine probability sample-based web surveys, there are several options available, but, because of their costs, these type of web surveys are less frequent. Couper (2000) identifies five different types of probability sample-based web surveys:

1. Intercept surveys. This type is the online equivalent of offline surveys based on systematic sampling, which is the selection of every kth element from a sampling frame or from a sequential

stream of potential respondents. The resulting sample is considered to be a probability sample as long as the sampling interval does not coincide with a pattern in the sequence being sampled and a random starting point is chosen. Online, this means systematically selecting visitors to a specific web page and recruiting them by pop-up invitations.

2. List-based samples. In this case, the sample is recruited from a list of people who form a well-defined population. Email lists as sampling frames are a common example, for instance to recruit members of an organization.

3. Mixed-mode surveys with Internet-based option. Traditional surveys can be combined with a web option, in which case a web survey is available to respondents of a traditionally selected probability sample. People are recruited by offline methods and the web is only a questionnaire delivery or dissemination option.

4. Pre-recruited online panels of Internet users. In this category are web surveys that use a panel made up of a probability sample of Internet users. These kinds of panel are representative of people with online access and often are maintained to be used in different studies – that is, not built up for just one study.

5. Pre-recruited online panels of the population. This is not only the most expensive but also the most complete option. A representative sample of the population is constructed using traditional sampling criteria (e.g. tax records as sampling frame), and Internet access is given to those who do not have it, thereby allowing them to respond to web surveys.

The above typology makes it clear that there is a multiplicity of options to carry out web surveys and, while the worries about coverage are understandable, they are mainly to do with resources. In other words, issues around coverage and sampling error are not very different from those connected to offline surveys. At the very beginning of the use of web surveys, non-probability samples and intercept or list-based samples were the most frequently used, probably because the panel-based options were very expensive. However, the relative costs of online panels of both Internet users and the general population are falling fast (mainly because providing Internet access to those who do not have it has become cheaper). There are some differences, depending of the geographical areas of the world in which we want to carry out our research: countries with large populations and low Internet penetration are the most difficult (as they are for traditional surveys).

Although the pre-recruited panels start as representative samples, non-response can jeopardize this representativeness. The recruitment process for such panels involves multiple steps, and potential panellists can drop out at any one of them. This leads to some of the problems related to web survey research that will be our next focus.

4.1.1 Intercept and systematic sampling

Intercept sampling on the web refers to the use of pop-up surveys or experiments that frequently use systematic sampling for every kth visitor to a website or web page. This sampling approach seems to be most useful as customer satisfaction or marketing online surveys. This type of systematic sampling can provide information that is generalizable to particular populations, such as those that visit a particular website/page. The data collection can be restricted to only those with certain IP (Internet Protocol) addresses, allowing one to target more specific subsets of visitors, and 'cookies' can be used to restrict the submission of multiple surveys from the same computer.

A potential issue with this type of data collection is non-response. Coomly (2000) reports typical response rates in the 15%–30% range, with the lowest response rates occurring for poorly targeted and/or poorly designed online surveys or experiments. The highest response rates were obtained for data collections that were relevant to the individual, either in terms of the particular survey questions or, in the case of marketing surveys, the commercial brand being surveyed.

As discussed in Couper (2000), an important issue with intercept sampling online is that there is no way to assess non-response bias, simply because no information is available on those that choose not to complete a study. Coomly (2000) hypothesizes that responses may be biased towards those who are more satisfied with a particular product, brand or website; towards those web browsers who are more computer and Internet savvy; and away from heavy Internet browsers who are conditioned to ignore pop-ups. Another source of non-response bias for intercept surveys implemented as pop-up browser windows may be pop-up blocker software, at least to the extent that pop-up blocker software is used differentially by various portions of the web-browsing community.

4.1.2 List-based samples

Sampling for Internet-based experiments, especially population-based survey experiments (PBSEs), using a list-based sampling frame can be conducted just as one would for a traditional survey using a sampling frame. Simple random sampling in this situation is straightforward to implement and requires nothing more than contact information (generally an email address for an online experiments) on each unit in the sampling frame. Of course, though only contact information is required to field the survey, having additional information about each unit in the sampling frame is desirable to assess (and perhaps adjust for) non-response effects.

While online experiments using list-based sampling frames can be conducted either via the web or by email, if an all-electronic approach is preferred, the invitation to take the study will almost always be made via email. And, because email lists of general populations are generally not available, this survey approach is most applicable to large homogeneous groups for which a sampling frame with email addresses can be assembled (e.g. universities, government organizations and large corporations). Couper (2000) calls these 'list-based samples' of high-coverage populations.

In more complicated sampling schemes, such as a stratified sampling, auxiliary information about each unit, such as membership in the relevant strata, must be available and linked to the unit's contact information. And more complicated multi-stage and cluster sampling schemes can be difficult or even impossible to implement for online experiments. To implement without having to directly contact respondents will likely require significant auxiliary data, which is unlikely to be available except in the case of specialized populations.

An example of multi-stage sampling procedure, used for online survey, applicable to the context of online experiments, of real-estate journalists for which no sampling frame existed, is reported by Jackob et al. (2005). For this study, the researchers first assembled a list of publications that would have journalists relevant to the study. From this list, a stratified random sample of publications was drawn, separately for each of five European countries. They then contacted the managing editor at each sampled publication and obtained the necessary contact information on all the journalists. All the journalists identified by the managing editors were then solicited to participate in a web survey. Jackob et al. (2005) concluded that it 'takes a lot of effort especially during the phase of preparation and planning' to assemble the necessary data and then to conduct an Internet-based survey using a multi-stage sampling methodology.

4.2 Static and adaptive design

Decades of research on survey methods inform current PBSE designs. Many surveys have similar designs and can benefit from each other. Online experiments in the form of PBSEs can benefit of the recent tendency in survey design of using an adaptive design or adaptive survey design (ASD). There are several reasons why this approach might be beneficial.

First, there is an uncertainty in how sample members respond to different design features. One way to view this source of uncertainty is in the form of *sample heterogeneity*. An example is with gaining cooperation, some people may be more likely to respond to altruistic reasons for participation in the online experiment, while others may respond to a particular incentive amount. Leverage-salience theory, first proposed by Groves et al. (2000) provides theoretical and empirical support for this heterogeneity. According to leverage-salience theory, different survey or experiment attributes such as the topic of the survey and the use of incentives have different leverages on a person's decision to participate. For one person, the topic of the survey may have a strong positive leverage, while for another, it may not have a strong leverage in their decision to participate – and may even have a negative leverage. Salience refers to how prominent this feature is made to the sample member. For someone for whom the topic of the survey has a strong positive leverage on their decision to participate, it would be essential to bring up the topic in contact materials, experiment introductions and other communication, in order to make it more salient relative to other features of the online experiment design. Yet, for the second person in this example, for whom the topic did not have a strong leverage or even had a negative leverage, exactly the opposite would be true – the topic of the survey has to be made less salient, and other features that have greater positive leverages (such as incentives) can be made more salient. This heterogeneity forms the basis for ASDs.

Second, researchers seldom know *what set of procedures will be most effective for an online survey or experiment*, prior to conducting the study. The choice of mode of data collection, contact protocol, incentive type, amount and timing are examples of major types of design decisions. Other content of the interviewer training and the text in the informed consent scripts are examples of more specific design choices. Taken together, researchers have a near infinite number of possible design combinations. The choice of design features can be informed by other surveys and reported experiments, but each study has unique aspects that limit the utility of past findings, leaving a degree of uncertainty about the optimal set of design features for a study. It may be near impossible to know whether to use a 10 Euro prepaid incentive at the onset of a study, 15 Euro prepaid incentive introduced at some point during the data collection period, 1 Euro prepaid incentive at the onset with a 25 Euros promised incentive offered late in the data collection period or a 50 Euro promised incentive used in a non-response follow-up phase, and these are just a limited set of possibilities based on a single design feature. Indeed, while many studies find that prepaid incentives yield higher response rates, some studies do not find the same result. This finding is not surprising as experiment design features interact with each other, and their effect is also conditional on what has occurred on the survey previously, the sequence of treatments. The conditional offer of an incentive can interact with the amount of the incentive, and both can have different effects on increasing participation depending on the mode and target population.

The paradigm of measuring the impact of a treatment is exactly what randomized controlled trials (RCTs) are designed to do as previously discussed. However, there are several challenges in applying the RCT framework to surveys and online experiments, which limits the applicability to other surveys and online experiments. RCTs typically involve a single treatment, while online experiment protocols can be seen as unique packages of treatments (e.g. pre-notification emails, model of data collection, level of interactivity protocols and topic of the experiment), the effects of which are unlikely to be independent. This may explain many contradictory findings in the scientific literature about single online experiment design features in isolation from their context.

Third, there is also *natural variability* that is often beyond researcher control: variability in the environment (e.g. the impact on online data collection outcomes during periods of intensive marketing season), variability in administering the protocol (e.g. different online platforms, devices used by respondents) and variability in sample composition (i.e. selecting a sample that may happen to be less cooperative relative to the rest of the sampling frame). These sources of variability are challenging to predict with any degree of certainty.

ASD has a role in addressing all three of these sources of uncertainty. Consider an online experiment in which the sample is heterogeneous with respect to how they respond to different protocols (e.g. mode, incentive amount), multiple protocols can be sequentially administered to sample members, and that some individuals in this sample seem to not respond to any protocol. One may want to use a design that builds on past data to identify what protocol works best on whom, what sequence, dosage (e.g. incentive amount) and timing of protocols to use on different groups in the sample, and maybe even use information collected during data collection to identify which sample elements are not worth pursuing further.

To better understand the nature of adaptive design, we can briefly summarize the typical steps of online survey design:

- Identify a general design to meet the study objectives (e.g. number of interviews, level of precision and time frame), for a given target population, within cost constraints. Make major decisions such as sampling frames, modes of contact and modes of interview.
- Develop the detailed study design, such as training protocols, contact materials, contact attempt rules and limits and incentive timing and amount. Make decisions among possible choices based on prior experience, research literature and subjective judgement.
- Develop the sampling design, to include assumed response rates and number of sample cases to be released.
- Collect the data. If any assumptions are found to be inaccurate and the objectives are not being met, develop remedies. An example is increasing the number of contact attempts and changing their scheduling, when a larger than expected proportion of the sample could not be contacted.
- Document any unplanned changes to data collection. If warranted, incorporate information about these changes into the weighting and estimation.

One striking aspect of this common approach to the design and conduct of surveys is that it largely ignores the first and second source of uncertainty – the unknown optimal set of design features and variability outside of researcher control. Uncertainty in data collection outcomes is seen as a nuisance factor, and when any of the assumptions that have gone into the design of the survey fail, *ad hoc* remedies are put into action. As the best design option among several choices may be unknown prior to data collection in the absence of experimental designs, decisions are made without direct evidence, guided only by existing literature and past experience. And regardless of the selected design, it may not perform as expected for any number or reasons, including the fact that the implementation of ad hoc changes is often hampered by time constraints that lead to suboptimal procedures. Could a researcher include multiple design options within the online experiment, to test alternatives or to simply have alternatives at the ready if needed?

A second aspect of major importance is the treatment of the sample as a homogenous group. By developing a single protocol (albeit with multiple design features) and administering it to each sample member, an implicit important assumption is that this protocol is more effective than alternative protocols, for the vast majority of the target population. Numerous studies have demonstrated this third source of uncertainty in survey data collection outcomes, such as identifying sample members who complete online surveys and experiments for altruistic reasons and others who are swayed by monetary incentives, and sample members who provide responses with less measurement error in one mode and others in a second mode. Could a researcher design different protocols to be used in an online experiment, to permit tailoring of procedures to the sample member? These last questions lead us to the motivation for ASDs. These designs are also aided by new opportunities posed by developments such as paradata, new sources of auxiliary data, real-time data collection systems and new analytic methods.

Paradata, first defined by Couper (1998), are data generated in the process of collecting data, such as clicks in a web survey, timestamps and outcome codes from each contact attempt. These data have grown in variety and ubiquity, particularly as a result of the intro-duction of computer-assisted interviewing, computer-administered survey modes and computerized sample management systems. These data can be useful for many purposes. For example, comput-erized data collection systems can capture each keystroke or selection, and timing data associated with each input. Changing responses and spending more time on questions have been found to be associated with survey responses in some studies (Heerwegh, 2003) and can be used to provide insight into how to improve survey instruments. The types of paradata are described in more detail in Chapter 5.

Auxiliary data are also increasing in variety and availability. For example, commercial data vendors can match household- and person-level data to sample telephone numbers and sample addresses, which in turn could be used to improve sampling designs and data collection procedures. These commercial auxiliary data often suffer from high levels of missingness, linkage error and measurement error, yet they could prove to be useful depending on the use – such as tailoring data collection procedures based on likely household composition and characteristics.

Real-time (and near real-time, such as daily updating) data collection systems offer an unprecedented ability to modify data collection procedures in response to outcomes. For example, simultaneous tracking of daily interaction hours, contact attempts, refusals and number of completed tasks can help inform when to stop a particular phase of data collection and switch to a different set of procedures. In addition to yielding more timely data, real-time data collection systems also provide the ability to change procedures faster, such as switching to another mode of data collection on the following day.

4.2.1 Adaptive versus responsive designs

Although primarily for simplicity of presentation the terms *adaptive survey design* and *responsive design* (RD) have been used interchangeably (Couper and Wagner, 2011), they do have different origins and, as a result, different meaning. *ASD* (Wagner, 2008) is based on the premise that samples are heterogeneous, and the optimal survey protocol may not be the same for each individual. A particular survey design feature such as incentives may appeal to some individuals, but not to others (Groves et al., 2000, 2006), leading to design-specific response propensity for each individual. Similarly, relative to interviewer administration, a self-administered mode of data collection may elicit less measurement error bias for some individuals, but more measurement error bias for others. The general objective in ASD is to tailor the protocol to sample members in order to improve targeted survey outcomes. The basic premise of adaptive interventions is shared by ASDs – tailoring methods to individuals based on interim outcomes. We label these *dynamic* adaptive designs to reflect the dynamic nature of the optimization and *static* adaptive designs when they are based solely on information available prior to the start of data collection. A tailoring variable is used to inform the decision to change treatments, such as the type of concerns the sample member may have raised at the doorstep. Decision rules would include the matching of information from the tailoring variables (concerns about time, not worth their effort) to interventions (a shorter version of the task, a larger incentive). Finally, the decision points need to be defined, such as whether to apply the rules and intervene at the time of the interaction or at a given point in the data collection period.

*RD*s are based on two major limitations of designing an online experiment protocol (mode, contact materials, number of contact attempts, incentives, etc.):

- Uncertainty about the best protocol, particularly as there are a near-infinite number of alternative combinations of design features.
- Using multiple protocols during the course of data collection may be more effective than using a single protocol, as in the case of non-response, different features can entice different people into participation.

As a result, RD refers to survey design with multiple phases, with each phase implementing a different protocol based on outcomes from prior phases. Unlike in ASD, the survey protocol used in each phase is not tailored to sample members, with the exception of random assignment to a control condition in order to evaluate which design is more effective in a given phase. Different protocols may be used in a single phase, but the goal is to compare designs and identify the preferred design for use in subsequent phases. Depending on the survey and the particular features of each phase, this also means that RD may require a longer data collection period than an adaptive design, as the latter can operate within a single phase.

RD is aimed at the identification of more effective protocols and sets of protocols to meet the study objectives, primarily within a single data collection. It has four distinct components:

1. Pre-identify a set of design features potentially affecting costs and errors of survey estimates.
2. Identify a set of indicators of the cost and error properties of those features and monitor those indicators in initial phases of data collection.
3. Alter the features of the survey in subsequent phases based on cost–error trade-off decision rules.
4. Combine data from the separate design phases into a single estimator.

The two designs are not mutually exclusive; rather, they can be complementary. For example, some surveys include multiple phases of data collection, each introducing a new set of design features, from changing incentive amounts to changing modes – a key characteristic of RD. Yet within each phase, not all sample members are subjected to the new protocol. Individuals or groups of individuals are identified based on the objectives of RD, such as those who are under-represented among the respondents in the prior phases and can be contributing to non-response bias, if not interviewed. Statistical models are often employed to identify which sample members should receive a different protocol in the following phase – a key characteristic of ASD.

4.3 Attrition in PBSE experiments

Attrition occurs when outcome data are missing. Certain forms of attrition pose a grave threat to unbiased inference. When attrition is systematically related to potential outcomes, removing observations from the dataset means that remaining subjects assigned to the treatment or control group no longer constitute random samples of the original collection of participants, and therefore a comparison of group averages may no longer be an unbiased estimator of the average treatment effect.

Why might an experiment fail to measure outcomes for some participants? The sources of attrition vary widely:

- Participants may refuse to cooperate with researchers. Experiments that measure outcomes using surveys routinely find that some participants are unwilling to fill out a post-treatment questionnaire.
- Researchers lose track of experimental participants. Substantial attrition often occurs, for example, when researchers investigate the long-term effects of an intervention using administrative data because participants change address or name.
- Firms, organizations or government agencies block researchers' access to outcomes. This problem is particularly common among experiments that focus on sensitive topics, such as corruption or electoral violence.
- The outcome variable may be intrinsically unavailable for some participants. For instance, an evaluation of a job training programme might aim to measure participants' wages six months later, but this outcome will go unmeasured for participants without jobs.
- Researchers deliberately discard observations. Perhaps ill-advisedly, laboratory researchers sometimes exclude from their analysis participants who seem not to understand the instructions or who fail to take the experimental situation seriously.

When attrition occurs, the researcher observes outcomes for certain participants and missing data for others. The researcher may choose to exclude participants with missing outcomes when analyzing the experimental results. This approach is risky. If attrition is systematically related to a participant's potential outcomes, analyzing the remaining observations may produce biased estimates of the average treatment effect.

Attrition forces the researcher to make assumptions about the statistical properties of missingness. One key issue is whether participants with missing outcomes have, on average, the same expected potential outcomes as participants for whom outcome data are available. When missingness is independent of potential outcomes, ignoring missing data and comparing group means will still yield unbiased inferences, although attrition reduces the effective sample size and thus increases standard errors. Because missing outcomes are, by definition, unavailable, one cannot directly assess whether missingness is systematically related to potential outcomes, although indirect evidence may be marshalled. Another modelling approach supposes that attrition is independent of potential outcomes within subgroups defined by the participants' background attributes. If attrition were unrelated to potential outcomes once we focus our attention on people with specified ages and levels of education, one could obtain unbiased estimates of average treatment effects by reweighting the data to 'fill in' the age/education cells that were depleted by attrition.

A second way to address the attrition problem is to guess the missing values of those who left the study. One approach is to explore worst-case scenarios, filling in the most extreme possible values – in effect, assuming that those who disappear from different experimental groups are extremely healthy or extremely ill. A related approach is to 'trim' the observations in the free care group, discarding its healthiest (or, conversely, its least healthy) participants until its attrition rate is as high as the attrition rate in the cost-sharing groups.

A final method for addressing attrition is to gather more data from missing participants. Because it may be prohibitively expensive to track down a large fraction of missing participants, particularly when the rate of missingness is high, there are research designs that focus on an intensive measurement effort on a random sample of those with missing outcomes.

Next, we will discuss the components that materially constitute an online experiment, those elements that can be not only objects of variation of design protocols, as discussed so far, but also a crucial complementary source of information, as in the case of metadata and paradata.

4.4 Chapter summary

In this chapter, we have discussed the following topics concerning sampling and online experiments:

- We have described the various forms of sampling that are employed in online experiments, in particular in PBSE. We identified five types of probability sample-based web surveys: (1) intercept surveys, (2) list-based samples, (3) mixed-mode surveys with Internet-based option, (4) pre-recruited online panels of Internet users and (5) pre-recruited online panels of the population. The latter is not only the most expensive but also the most complete option. A representative sample of the population is constructed using traditional sampling criteria (e.g. tax records as sampling frame), and Internet access is given to those who do not have it, thereby allowing them to respond to web surveys.

- The next step was introducing the notion of ASD. The general objective in ASD is to tailor the protocol to sample members to improve targeted survey outcomes. The basic premise of adaptive interventions is shared by ASDs – tailoring methods to individuals based on interim outcomes. We label these dynamic adaptive designs to reflect the dynamic nature of the optimization and static adaptive designs when they are based solely on information available before the start of data collection.

- The last part of this chapter focussed on the role of attrition in online experiments. Attrition occurs when outcome data are missing. Certain forms of attrition pose a grave threat to unbiased inference. When attrition is systematically related to potential outcomes, removing observations from the dataset means that remaining subjects assigned to the treatment or control group no longer constitute random samples of the original collection of participants, and therefore a comparison of group averages may no longer be an unbiased estimator of the average treatment effect.

Further readings

Currently, there are no specific books about the issue of sampling in online experiments, and the use of online experiments using online panels is simply very novel at this stage. However, several texts are still useful because they focus on the sampling of web surveys. Among these books, the most useful in their applications to online experiments are as follows:

- a comprehensive and technical text about almost all aspects of sampling is Lohr's *Sampling: Design and Analysis* (2021);
- one text that deals specifically with online panels is the edited book by Callegaro et al. (2014), *Online Panel Research: A Data Quality Perspective*, and it deals with the online panels' quality issues such as attrition and the complexity of non-response in probability-based online panel for the general population (those that we would normally use for online experiments);
- and more recently, there is the guide by Eichhorn, *Survey Research and Sampling* (2022), that provides an overview of the different sampling issues in survey research, including the online.

More specific to online sampling, there is also:

- Toepoel's *Doing Surveys Online* (2016), which contains a section about the use of online panels;
- and last is the great effort by Fielding, Lee and Blank, who edited *The SAGE Handbook of Online Research Methods* (2017) although there is no section about online experiments, there is a chapter dedicated to online sampling for surveys.

5

BUILDING YOUR EXPERIMENT

- Metadata comprise information collected along with the experiment responses and the actual answers.
- Paradata are empirical measurements about the process of creating the experiment data; they refer to recordings about the fieldwork process. Paradata can be *directly* recorded – in this case, we talk of direct paradata. They are an integral part of available software to develop and carry out online experiments. *Indirect paradata* are those collected by adding instruments, for example, eye-tracking devices, skin conductance setups, video recording systems, etc.
- The length of an online experiment interacts with its design and, most notably, with the choice of a between-participants or within-participants design.
- Visual dynamic stimuli presented on screen in an online experiment are constrained by the *refresh rate* of screens.
- There are two types of mouse inputs that are useful in online experiments: *mouse clicks and mouse movements*. Mouse clicks are the most straightforward type of input because they can be associated not only with the selection of options on the screen but also with other types of interaction. Mouse movements can be used as proxy of participants' attention and visualized using heat maps.
- Using smart devices like smartphone and smartwatch, we can identify four main types of sensors: *physical sensing, cognitive sensing, emotional sensing* and *social sensing*.

5.1 Affordances and interface design choices

The design of online experiments requires careful design choices not only from the perspective of the methodological and statistical design, what we have discussed in the previous sections, but also about the use of interfaces and their affordances. The notion of affordance (Gibson, 1977) elaborated by Donald Norman (1999) in the context of design refers to the concept of affordances to refer to the perceivable actionable properties of objects. For instance, a chair could be considered to afford sitting, a knob to afford turning and so on. Because in online experiments, the screen of a computer, tablet or smartphone is the main point of interaction between the researcher and the participants, all aspects need to be considered. In the author's experience, the first information to gather concerns the nature of the most common type of device that members of the study will use to enter and participate in our online experiment.

This information is not always available, but there are two potential scenarios and relative strategies. The first scenario is when we use online panels as the pool to recruit our participants. This is the most straightforward case because the maintainers of the online panel usually know a great deal of information about its members' characteristics, including using different digital devices used to participate in online studies. For example, finding out if people use more a tablet, a smartphone or a larger screen can help us know vital information concerning design choices that we will discuss later. Moreover, it tells us about the environmental conditions in which participants might complete the study. Using highly mobile devices such tablets and smartphones could indicate that participants might join the study outside their homes. Different devices have consequences on at least four elements of the design of online experiment:

1 Screen 'real estate' size and the presentation of visual stimuli, from pictures, videos to text.
2 The input device used by the participants, a keyboard or a mouse, is different from a touchscreen.
3 The use of sound and audio stimuli might be affected by the device used.
4 The collection of metadata and paradata can be influenced by the type of device used by participants.

In the following discussions, let us briefly discuss the four points mentioned above that will be reconsidered in the more specific discussion of the interface elements.

The screen real estate is an essential factor considering that it is the main constrain in vehiculating a certain amount of information to participants but intervenes in whichever task we ask participants to do. In designing online experiments that comprised classification tasks, the author experience is that often the researcher faces the problem of designing different modalities of participants' interaction depending on the type of device used. However, the different modalities of interaction can play a confounding factor in the experiment, so it needs to be accounted for. When experiments concern cognitive tasks, the different affordance of interfaces is likely to play a role.

Different devices allow different uses of audio stimuli. While it is possible to have good quality audio on portable devices using headphones, a further screening requirement needs to be factored in if audio is important in the experiment at hand. While we tend to picture the ideal scenario of a participant at home in front of a PC screen and with either speakers or headphones, a growing number of participants in online panels use mobile devices. We cannot make precise statements about what proportion is likely to be found, but in the author's experience, this ranges from 15% to 30%.

The last point to discuss is the collection of metadata and paradata. In general, the main source of metadata and paradata is the platform used to implement and carry on our online experiment. There are several platforms, each with their pro and cons, and we will discuss them later. However, all of them share those participants, through a web browser app, and land on the platform, which can record several metadata and paradata (we will discuss them later).

If participants use mobile devices, particularly smartphones, there is an additional potential source of metadata and paradata: the device itself. Smartphones contain an increasingly complex array of sensors that collect information that could be useful for this purpose; we will discuss these in a subsequent dedicated session of this chapter.

5.1.1 Interface

Online experiment design exploits a wide range of visual features, so respondents are likely to use the visual features of the questions or response options as supplementary information to help them pin down the meaning of the question or the potential answers. Many experiment items use partially labelled response scales for attitudinal items and the respondents may have difficulty in assigning precise meanings to the scale points, particularly those that are not labelled verbally. Therefore, there are many aspects of design to be considered to account for potential medium effects given the rich set of options at our disposal. The first issue concerns the basic layout of an online experiment: *the scrolling versus paging approach* (Figure 5.1).

Most online experiments and surveys have more text than can be fitted onto a single screen. By *screen*, I mean here the physical device on which the browser displays the webpage and therefore our questionnaire. The term *page* in the context of web survey design has a different meaning from its equivalent on paper: in the digital context, the page is synonymous with document and can be the size of a single screen or many screens. Most websites, for example, have a home page and many other pages or HTML documents that one can navigate to with the aid of hyperlinks. In addition, we often talk of forms: a *form* is a specific type of page.

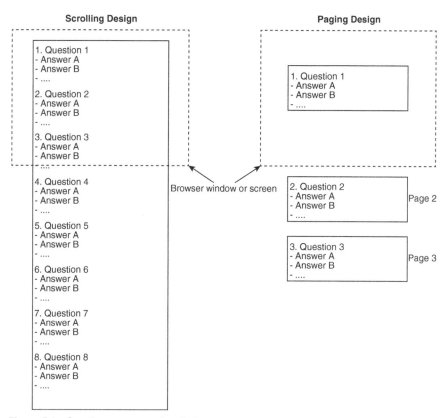

Figure 5.1 Scrolling versus paging design

Compared to pages that are typically static, in that they are designed for the display of text and images, forms are interactive.

The difference between scrolling and paging designs of web surveys is a continuum rather than a binary choice. It ranges from scrolling designs where the entire survey is a single web form to paging designs where each question is presented on a separate web form. In the prototypical version of the scrolling design approach, the entire questionnaire is contained in a single HTML form, with one or more action buttons (e.g. submit, cancel) at the very end. This approach is most like a paper-based self-administered survey, where routing is not automated and minimized, and respondents can browse back and forth through the instrument, answering questions in any order, changing answers at will and answering all or some of the questions before submitting the response.

The advantages of a scrolling design are as follows:

- Participants can easily assess the length of the questionnaire and review forthcoming questions scrolling down.
- It tends to be easier for respondents to review their questions because they are free to move back and forth throughout the webpage: they can answer questions in any order they prefer. It means that the reviewing of answers is somewhat encouraged by the design.
- This design is easy to program from the point of view of the researcher and is less exposed to potential technical difficulties (e.g. improper routing, partial loading of forms). There is less interaction with the server, reducing the likelihood of failures or errors during transmission.
- Given that the instruments are simpler, and no complex code is involved, the downloading of a static instrument may be marginally faster than a comparable interactive survey.

The scrolling design has also some drawbacks, given its relatively simple design:

- Because of its design, a pure scrolling design implies that the questionnaire has to be completed in one session. It is possible to carry out additional programming to allow a 'save and complete later' option, but this is not normally available.

- Respondents can see all the questions, including those not relevant for them. However, this might be a problem for some questionnaires, especially those in which a given order of response is required and where routing and skipping are included. For some types of survey, the researcher needs to be able to control the order in which the questions are answered (e.g. contingent questions, attitude measure scales) (Malhotra, 2009).
- Routing of participants and skipping of parts of the questionnaire are more difficult to engineer, thereby increasing the chance of errors.
- Several interactive features are either not available or difficult to implement, such as dynamically generated fills, customized question text and randomization of questions or response options.
- Scrolling tends to require greater dexterity and hand–eye coordination, particularly for longer surveys. One side effect is that it may increase the likelihood of missed items and unanswered questions.

The relative importance of each of these issues depends on the goals or features of the overall survey design. That is, what kinds of questions are to be asked; what expectations exist about the knowledge, experience and motivation of the respondents; how long and/or complex the instrument is and so on.

The alternative to a scrolling design is the paging approach. In this type of design, the survey is divided into several sets of web forms, each of which contains one or more questions. At the extreme, this may involve a single question per screen but most commonly more questions are present. The instrument is often designed so that each form occupies a single screen, obviating the need for scrolling. In other words, groups of questions, which constitute a form, are paginated and each form fits the average computer screen. This approach permits customization of question text, randomization, automated skips and routing, edits and many more features.

Some of the advantages of the paging design approach are as follows:

- Minimal use of scrolling and focussing. Because each webpage contains a limited set of questions, there is a very limited use of scrolling and attention is therefore more focussed on the group of questions available on each screen. This might be a particularly desirable feature if the questions require high cognitive effort.
- Routing and skips can be automated, allowing complex combinations to be implemented and removing from the respondent the burden of worrying about which questions to answer.
- Partially completed questionnaires can be retained and completed later if needed.
- Immediate feedback for groups of questions can be provided on their dedicated page, including further explanations.

Paging design is a more feature-rich version of web surveys, but it comes with some potential disadvantages as well:

- More programming is needed for this kind of design and that means higher costs because it requires either custom-built solutions or specialized software.
- Respondents have less control about the order of answers and reviewing their previous questions is discouraged compared to scrolling designs, even if it is made possible by use of a simple 'back button'.
- From a technical point of view, paging designs, because of their more flexible interactive features, are also more dependent on interactions with the server hosting the webpages and are therefore more prone to problems related to transmissions failures.

Research has been done in comparing the two approaches (Norman et al., 2001; Peytchev et al., 2006; Tourangeau et al., 2004). Overall, the difference between the two in terms of omissions and errors is not very large, although the paging approach is more likely to err in this direction, but it depends very much on the other features that might be present in a web survey. The choice between two approaches can be done only by taking in consideration all aspects of the intended web survey design; there are, however, some basic guidelines that can be a starting point. The scrolling design is well suited when (1) the survey is short; (2) no routing and skips are required; (3) the order of answers is not a concern; (4) respondents' ability to review previous answers is desirable; and (4) missing and incomplete data are not a main concern.

5.1.1.1 Colours, fonts and layout

Online experiments, much like online surveys, contain many other design features besides their general layout. We have mentioned slides, drag and drop options, etc. Web surveys are interactive and rich visual tools. An important distinction is between the design elements related to the task and the broader style elements. The task elements are those parts of the survey instrument that are directly related to the task of completing the survey. These include the survey questions, the response options and the buttons used to move through the survey. Web surveys also contain style elements. These are the parts of the instrument that are orthogonal or incidental to the task itself and may include the overall design of the site (e.g. the colour scheme, typography), branding elements (logos, contact information) and auxiliary functions such as help, progress indicators and so on. While there are many potential style elements, let us consider two main issues: colour and text.

Regarding colour, it is not so much an issue of aesthetics and of a visually pleasing design, but we should be aware of the possible effects of colour choices or decisions on respondents. Colour is important for several reasons:

- Some people are colour blind and may not be able to distinguish among different colours.
- The choice of colour may affect contrast and aspects of readability of the verbal information presented.

- Colour conveys meaning and may affect the answers respondents give in direct or indirect ways.
- If different colours are used in a web survey, respondents will assume that the colours have meaning.

Besides the issue of accessibility for colour-blind participants, the cultural meaning (Madden et al., 2000; Wierzbicka, 1992) and psychological effect of colours (Weller and Livingston, 1988) should be considered. Regarding the first, cultural variation in the associated meaning of colours can be a problem in international studies with a cross-cultural nature.

Other style elements that deserve attention are fonts because of the role that they can have in terms of cognitive load to participants. Because web surveys are displayed on a monitor, font types that work well on paper can be difficult to read on screen, and font sizes on screen are different from front sizes on paper. Readability is the main concern regarding fonts because it can have effects on the perceived difficulty of a task (Song and Schwarz, 2008) and, therefore, potentially influence participants' performance. A common web design rule is that *sans serif* fonts (e.g. Helvetica, Avenir) are clearer online than *serif* fonts (e.g. Times New Roman, Palatino, Garamond), which look better on paper. Since researchers cannot foresee which type of screen or computer will be used by participants to answer a web survey, it is better to be aware that font sizes on some operating systems are different from font sizes on others.

As mentioned before, a further complication rises if an online experiment is meant to be accessed by other devices such as tablets and smartphones. A dynamic layout that adjusts itself depending on the type of device used by participants is preferable, but decisions made about scrolling and paging design need to be updated considering such diversity.

The visual aspects of task elements are fundamental because in web surveys, many different styles can be implemented. While such richness is welcome, using extravagant solutions for the sake of aesthetics or simply novelty is a risk. The role of visual design choices in scales, midpoints, spacing of polarities, etc. can affect respondents. For example, in the absence of conflicting information, they may assume that the scale options are supposed to represent equally spaced points on the underlying dimension of judgement. This expectation is defined as the *presumption of equal spacing*. Similarly, when the scale is clearly bipolar (say, one endpoint is labelled 'Very strongly agree' and the other endpoint is labelled 'Very strongly disagree'), respondents may assume that the scales points are intended to represent points that are symmetrically arrayed around a neutral midpoint on the underlying continuum. This issue is referred as the *presumption of symmetry* (which applies only to bipolar scales).

According to Tourangeau et al. (2004), respondents apply five heuristics that help them interpret the response scales in web and other visual surveys. Each heuristic assigns a meaning to some visual feature of the response scale or of the item itself. The five most common heuristics are as follows:

1 Middle means typical or central.
2 Left and top mean first.
3 Near means related.
4 Like (in appearance) means close (in meaning).
5 Up means good.

The first point stresses the importance of the visual midpoint of a scale because it anchors the meaning of other scale points. According to the presumption of symmetry, the midpoint of a bipolar scale will be considered the conceptual midpoint of the latent dimension measured, in other words a neutral point. In the case of unipolar scale, respondents might interpret it as midpoint in terms of being the median or mode. The second heuristic refers to the expectation that respondents tend to have about a logical order of response options. In a horizontal arrangement, the leftmost option is assumed to be the first moving to the rightmost. In a vertical arrangement, the top option is considered the starting point moving to the bottom (Tourangeau et al., 2004). The 'Near means related' heuristic refers to the tendency for respondents to infer a conceptual relation between two items based on their physical proximity. The fourth heuristic refers to the tendency for respondents to infer conceptual similarity between two items or response options based on their similarity in appearance. For example, when the two ends of the response scale are shades of the same hue, respondents may infer that the two extremes are closer conceptually than when the two ends of the scales are shades of the different hues. The fifth heuristic, 'Up means good', involves inferring something about the value of an item from its position on the screen. We argue that vertical position and desirability (Christian et al., 2007) are often linked metaphorically (e.g. heaven is above, hell below; upswings are good, downswings bad; an upbeat mood is positive, a downbeat mood negative).

It is most likely that, as new visual features become available for web survey design, additional heuristics will play a role in shaping respondents' answers. Researchers ought to consider design aspects, both style and task elements, as much as they do the crafting of questions and scales themselves. Recent advancements in bounded rationality-related research have increased our knowledge of the subtle interference played by visual cues, heuristics and general unconscious influences that might affect respondents.

5.2 Metadata and paradata

Online experiments are characterized by another aspect beside their visual features and interactivity: not only the possibility of collecting data by means of tasks and questions but also the use of the overall experiment and fieldwork process. While this information was in theory possible to obtain in lab experiments, it was very difficult to collect. Lab experiments, especially computer-assisted ones, made the use of metadata and paradata more available and increasingly important. Online experiments are packed with this additional type of information that can play either a complementary role or a more crucial one in a researcher's analysis. We can distinguish between three categories of information that we can collect using an online experiment: the main data (experiment data); the metadata (data about data) and the paradata (data about the process of collecting data).

Metadata comprise information collected along with the experiment responses in addition to the actual answers. Metadata can be used to analyze participation information both to improve response rates in a live experiment and to inform future experiment plans. Examples of online experiments metadata are:

- time taken to complete the experiment,
- channel by which participant accessed the experiment,
- response rate for the experiment,
- participation trend over time and
- language in which experiment was completed.

Paradata are empirical measurements about the process of creating the experiment data; they refer to recordings about the fieldwork process. Online experiments offer the possibility of capturing rich paradata with relative ease. Paradata can be directly recorded – in this case, we talk of direct paradata. They are an integral part of available software to develop and carry out online experiment. Indirect paradata are those collected by adding instruments, for example, eye-tracking devices, skin conductance setups and video recording systems.

Direct paradata can be grouped in three categories: paradata about contact info, paradata about device type and paradata about the experimental task navigation and interaction. The first type of direct paradata often concerns the researcher's actions (about contacting and recruiting participants), while the second and third groups are more related to respondents' actions.

Contact info paradata are most like those already collected in telephone and face-to-face interviews, the 'call record paradata'. This information is about the contact tries to get respondents. In online experiments, the ability to trace this kind of information has been greatly improved compared to the past and it is borrowed by the extensive use of web surveys. An example of contact info paradata is the outcomes of email invitations – whether they were received, read, deleted or even marked as spam. Another example is the information about access to the experiment introduction, which is important because it allows researchers to calculate response rates for the online experiment. Similarly, paradata about the last task or question answered before dropping out of the experiment are also vital to determine the eligibility of the unit/respondent for further analysis and help improve the dropout problem.

Original to online surveys and experiments are paradata about the device used by respondents. While many pieces of information can be gathered in this context, three are of particular importance. Paradata about screen sizes, resolution and type of device help researchers to identify potential problems with the visual layout of an online experiment, as discussed before. Another important piece of information concerns what multimedia content is supported by participants' devices, which is useful to avoid technical problems of delivering content. The third important device-related paradata are the so-called 'cookies' and IP recordings. The latter information can be used to avoid multiple entries and check for duplicates because these paradata are unique for each respondent.

The last and larger family of direct paradata concerns information about the interaction between respondents and the experimental tasks and the way in which they navigated and answered (Heerwegh, 2003). Examples of this type of paradata are:

- time spent per screen (in the case of a paging design),
- response latency,
- keystrokes and mouse clicks,
- reviews of answers and
- validation and warning messages.

The first two bits of information can play a very important role in quality control. Information about time spent on screen and response latencies can also be used to understand the level of cognitive effort (Yan and Tourangeau, 2008) or ambiguity of questions (Heerwegh, 2003). The same information is used to detect respondents who have very short response latency, which might signal the fact that they are not properly reading the questions: these respondents are known as 'speeders' (Zhang and Conrad, 2014). Many market research companies use this information to screen out data from respondents classified as speeders and, therefore, as fake respondents. However, the use of this information is not simple and various measures and metrics continue to be developed (Zhang and Conrad, 2013). Paradata about keystrokes and mouse clicks are a further evolution of the previous example and are particularly suited to web surveys that contain highly interactive material that involves typing and mouse actions. Moreover, tracking mouse movements is used as a means of tracking people's gaze and visualizing 'heat maps' of interaction (Freeman and Ambady, 2010).

Changing or revising answers comprises another type of paradata that can be used as an indicator for spotting potentially confusing or ambiguous questions. Depending of the importance of the response order and the way in which this has been implemented in the design (possible, facilitated, discouraged), such paradata information are particularly important for attitudinal and opinion-based questions (Stieger and Reips, 2010). The last example of paradata about navigation concerns the use of validation and error messages created by incorrect interaction of respondents with questions (e.g. an invalid entry or a missing answer). Such information can be used to develop a quality index to improve a web survey design further.

Paradata collection is increasingly more embedded in many online experiments platforms, although there are differences in terms of basic or more advanced paradata collected. Researchers can develop their own scripts to collect such information, but available tools are usually sufficient. Another aspect to consider is that when paradata contain personal information, such data are protected by law and, therefore, require specific treatment. For example, information concerning IP addresses compromises the anonymity of data. Paradata also raises ethical concerns and practical dilemmas about how to inform respondents about their collection. The EU's General Data Protection Regulation requires explicit consent and a clear explanation of the type of data, metadata and paradata collected from each user and how they will be used. Compared to the recent past, privacy and data protection regulations are now more restrictive and precise. Legal and ethical viability and validation should be considered an essential part of the research process from the very start.

5.3 Length

The length of your online experiment largely depends on the tasks that it entails. There are, however, some aspects to consider that are common to all designs. The first consideration is practical. In this book, we adopt the population-based survey experiments as the best example of carrying out online experiments for the reasons previously discussed in terms of external validity. One consequence of this methodological choice is that we rely on online pre-recruited panels that are accessed not for free in almost the totality of cases (it is simply not feasible for researchers to build and maintain their own pre-recruited online panel). The cost of recruiting participants using existing online pre-recruited panels depends on several factors, one very important is the duration of the participation. In the author's experience, the duration of 20 minutes is considered the industry baseline from which the costs increased considerably for more extended involvement. In other words, most online experiments tend to be designed so that participants can complete them within 20 minutes, including the option of answering several questionnaire-like items for profiling purposes.

Therefore, the pragmatic choice is to contain the duration of the experiment with 20 minutes more or less. Online experiments of 25–30 minutes are also common.

The second reason has to do with the nature of an online experiment, where our degree of control on the participants' level of attention is significantly reduced at the benefit of a larger and more diverse sample directly reached online. An extended online experiment increases the likelihood of people's distractions, cognitive fatigue and other potential problems. While there is some evidence that some ambience noise and disturbance are not problematic (see

Wenz, 2021), longer experimental tasks increase the chances of environmental confounding. While researchers have developed ways of controlling for the level of attention using attention check items (Shamon and Berning, 2020), longer tasks tend to degrade cognitive resources over time, especially when complex tasks are requested. Cognitive fatigue does affect visual selective attention (Faber et al., 2012), and in the context of the visual-dominant type of experiments, the risk of fatigue should be minimized.

The length of an online experiment interacts with its design and, most notably, with the choice of a between-participants or within-participants design. In the first case, the between-participants design option is the one that minimizes length because of the presence of several independent treatment groups. The within-participants design is the option that allows savings in the number of respondents, but it increases the experiment's length. An online experiment with many tasks and within-participants design is the scenario most at risk of cognitive fatigue. As discussed in previous sections, the same scenario is also at risk of programming errors because complex blocking is necessary to account for order effects.

In summary, there are limitations to the extent of how long an online experiment can last. Lab experiments can last longer, although the issue of costs and cognitive fatigue does not disappear in that context. Therefore, online experiments are a compromise in terms of length, which is balanced by the other gains in terms of numerosity, diversity and extension of the sample of participants involved.

5.4 Timing and dynamic stimuli

A different topic from length is the issue of timing and dynamic stimuli in online experiments. While in lab experiments, the matter of timing in both the presentation of stimuli and the recording of reactions can be achieved with the support of specific hardware, in online experiments, we need to rely on software solutions and some critical considerations about the use of screens.

Briefly, the issue is that your monitor operates at a fixed screen refresh rate (typically 60 Hz, so each 'frame' lasts for 1/60th of a second or 16.667 ms). Stimuli cannot be drawn for a duration that is not a whole number of frames; either they appear on that screen refresh or they do not. The best way to present brief stimuli with very precise timing is to time their appearance in terms of the number of the frame on which they appear or disappear. For this to work, you do need to know the refresh rate of your monitor and that the computer is set to synchronize with the monitor refresh. Most computers will be synchronizing correctly by default, and most standard monitors are running at a 60 Hz refresh rate.

The previous generation of computer screens was based on the cathode ray tube (CRT) technology. However, most 'flat' screens that you encounter will be liquid crystal display (LCD) panels (there are also LED screens around, but those are still a minority as computer monitors, and we will not talk about them here). Most projectors also use LCD panels and have exactly the same properties and caveats as below. LCDs work by a different technology to CRT displays. Unlike the pixels in the CRT, which light up, these pixels are more like a colour filter and need a light behind them (a 'backlight'). Unlike the array of pixels of a CRT that briefly flash on as the electron beam passes over them, this backlight is always on (in standard consumer systems). Also, the pixel does not have a black period between each screen refresh – it merely switches to the next colour, as needed in the next frame.

Traditionally, the pixel colour switching rate was rather sluggish compared with CRTs; it took longer for the liquid crystal to change colour than it did for the CRT phosphor to light up. For many years, this was a problem for scientists (particularly vision scientists) because the stimulus would 'persist' after it had been removed from the screen, and objects that moved would leave a trail behind them. Luckily those days are gone; modern LCD panels have very fast switching times and are now very suitable high-speed displays for many scientific experiments. LCDs have the problem that they nearly all have a fixed refresh rate (mostly 60 Hz but 120 and 240 Hz monitors are also now available) and that the screen fills downwards from the top rather than updating everywhere simultaneously. One concern with LCD panels, though, and this can be quite a major problem for precisely timed studies, is that some of these screens do not just present the screen pixels exactly as sent by the graphics card but perform some post-processing on them to make the colours more vivid or the blacks more black. The first problem with this is that you, the scientist, might have spent a long time perfectly calibrating your stimuli only to have them altered by the monitor. However, the worse problem is that it might not manage to do this reliably within the frame period. This means that, although you managed to send the pixels for your screen update in time and correctly reported the time that the computer updated its output, the screen itself was delayed in displaying that stimulus. For this reason, if the precise time that a stimulus appears matters to you, then you might want to test this with some form of light detector that tells you about your stimulus timing (e.g. Cedrus StimTracker). On the plus side, having determined that your monitor itself is not introducing timing errors, it should remain that way; it should not, for instance, only have erratic timing when certain stimuli are presented.

Another critical thing to know about your LCD panel is that it has a 'native' resolution and, although it might be willing to accept other resolutions as inputs, it must ultimately present the screen image at its native resolution. If your computer's monitor settings do not agree with the native resolution of the panel, it will interpolate the pixel values to fit. In extreme cases, where the aspect ratio doesn't match, this will cause the screen image to look stretched on the monitor, but in nearly all cases, it will result in blurring. This will be most visible around sharp, narrow edges, such as pieces of text, but it will occur over the whole screen. To ensure your screen image is as sharp as possible, always check to set your stimuli to a resolution that is acceptable to the most common screen resolution available to participants.

The last notable difference between CRT and LCD technology, but probably only important to vision scientists, is that LCD panels are not analogue devices with a continuous range of luminance values like CRT displays. Instead, they have a fixed set of values, most commonly 256 possible levels for each colour channel (this system has 8 bits per channel). Some LCD panels, especially on laptops, will only provide 6 bits (only 64 levels of each gun) and then apply fancy technology (dithering) to try and get intermediate colours. A few LCD panels allow a larger 10-bit range (1,024 grey levels).

Considering what type of visualization your participants will experience is essential if visual static and dynamic stimuli play an important role in your experiment. In summary:

- The screen no longer flashes between black and the target colour; it always stays 'on' and merely switches directly from one colour to the appropriate colour for the next frame.
- The updating of pixels still typically occurs from the top to the bottom of the screen and still takes the majority of the screen refresh period to update the lines of the screen incrementally.
- Flat panels are not analogue devices; they have a fixed number of luminance levels, most commonly 256.
- Flat panels have a 'native' resolution, and setting the computer to output at any other resolution simply requires the monitor to interpolate the image back to that native resolution.
- The physical requirement of the timing of frames is less strict for flat panels, but currently, most monitors still have a fixed, whole-screen refresh cycle in keeping with the CRT technology they supersede.

Next, we move to the use of mouse data as a source of information.

5.5 Mouse data as input

In most scenarios, participants to our online experiments will interact with our tasks using a keyboard and a mouse\trackpad. Broadly speaking, there are two types of mouse inputs that are useful in online experiments: mouse clicks and mouse movements. Mouse clicks are the most straightforward type of input because they can be associated not only with the selection of options in the screen but also with other type of interaction, for example, drag and drop an item from one part to another of the screen.

We will look at the potential insights from the mouse movements and heat maps (Figure 5.2). The main metrics implemented in mouse tracking tools are based on the analysis of individual mouse trajectories during the reaction of a participant in an experimental trial. Existing tools compute basic and derived (e.g. minimum, maximum or standard deviations) values connected to mouse trajectories. Specifically, these metrics involve values related to mouse positions (including the extraction of mouse positions without mouse movements), reaction time, directional changes, velocity and acceleration. Moreover, mouse tracking analysis examines the deviation of the produced trajectories from the theoretical optimal ones, which correspond to straight lines. This deviation can be illustrated by

Figure 5.2 Example of mouse heat map

computing metrics such as maximum absolute deviation, area under curve and maximum deviation. The behaviour examination of experimental participants (or users for the case of usability studies) could also be enhanced by the visual exploration of different visualizations of the produced trajectories on the visual stimuli. Despite the existing software solutions implementing and supporting specific and advanced metrics to reveal visual behaviour, the relative techniques for data visualization can be improved. Moreover, the development of 'cumulative' metrics that indicate the overall visual behaviour could help towards modelling this behaviour as well as for training models towards predicting participant/user reaction.

Furthermore, raw data produced by mouse tracking techniques meet several similarities with eye-tracking data considering both their spatiotemporal distribution and their connection with the perceptual and cognitive processes. Scientific literature shows that there is a strong correlation between mouse and eye movements (Johnson et al., 2012), while there are also research studies trying to predict the gaze behaviour using mouse movements, but these types of techniques are not without methodological issues. In their systematic review, Schoemann and colleagues (Schoemann et al., 2021, p. 16) state that 'Mouse cursor tracking is exquisitely sensitive to a range of design features and to enhance the potential of this method to explore cognition, we need to be clear about the implications of our design choices'.

Information about mouse movements is often represented using heat maps. A heat map (or heatmap) is a graphical representation of data where values are depicted by colour. When people say 'heat map', they typically mean hover map. It shows you areas that people have hovered over with their mouse cursor – and the idea is that people look where they hover, so it is kind of like poor man's eye-tracking. The heat map is really an umbrella term for different heat mapping tools: scroll maps, click maps and move maps.

Scroll maps are one type of heat map, where the 'hottest' colours show the most viewed sections of the page, rather than the most clicked (or tapped) elements of it. In other words, scroll maps generate heat zones of your website or app pages from top to bottom, so they look more like a vertical rainbow instead of depicting the 'confetti' patterns typical of other types of heat maps like click or move maps.

Click maps are another specific type of heat map where the red or 'hot' dots show page elements that have been clicked on most frequently, while blue or 'cold' dots show the ones that have been clicked on the least. Any area that contains no colour has never been clicked on.

Move maps track where desktop users move their mouse as they navigate the page. The hot spots in a move map represent where users have moved their cursor on a page, and research suggests a correlation between where people are looking and where their mouse is – meaning that a move map gives you an indication of where people might be looking as they go through your page.

Overall, mouse data can be very informative both as paradata of our online experiments or as an integral part of it. In both cases, however, the use of a mouse is related to the existing assumption that the dominant modality of fruition of our online experiment might be through a PC. However, the role of other types of devices also for the data collection using online experiments is very much on the rise.

5.6 Using mobile and tablet sensors

The recent technological advances enabled the release of smart-phone devices with powerful specifications and enormous sensing possibilities. These devices have been increasingly used in health-care and behavioural research in order to collect health data and deliver comprehensive healthcare information to practitioners, researchers and patients, by enhancing the ability to diagnose and track diseases. Tablets can be considered the same type of smart-phone because they usually contain a subset of the sensors available to a smartphone, but it largely depends on the model and age of the device (a new iPad with cellular capacity is indistinguishable in terms of sensors from an iPhone).

We can, instead, distinguish by type of sensors available and their domain of data in the context of the study of human behaviour. We identify four groups of sensors:

1 *Physical sensing* can be achieved using accelerometer, gyroscope, GPS, magnetometer, Bluetooth and microphone audio.
2 *Cognitive sensing* can be carried out using screen status, SMS, accelerometer, GPS, Wi-Fi, Bluetooth and phone activity.
3 *Emotional sensing* can be performed using microphone audio, SMS, phone activity, accelerometer, GPS, Wi-Fi, Bluetooth, phone activity and experience sampling method.
4 *Social sensing* can be done using microphone audio, social media activity, phone calls and SMS and Bluetooth.

Let us discuss each in turn, we start with physical sensing.

Physical sensing. The research on physical activity recognition has gained much attention during the recent years as an essential descriptor of human behaviour. For more than two decades, researchers have intensively explored the use of inertial sensors, such as accelerometers and gyroscopes, to fairly quantify physical activity in epidemiological, surveillance and intervention medicine. These devices fundamentally consist of an accelerometer, a small inertial sensor that records the movement of the body where the device is placed (e.g. wrist, arm, chest, hip, thigh). Smartphones, which natively incorporate these types of inertial sensors, have been studied for estimating human physical activity in both controlled and uncontrolled settings.

The use of mobile phones as stand-alone physical activity monitors has been explored during the last decade, as a technological follow-up of traditional accelerometer-based mechanisms. The first systems on physical activity monitoring through mobile phones were based on simple pedometers and step counters building on the acceleration measured through the built-in sensors. However, the use of more sophisticated machine learning techniques has enabled the extraction of more meaningful data for activity detection. For example, sedentary, ambulatory and commuting activities (e.g. walking, jogging, running, cycling, ascending/descending stairs, sitting, standing) have been successfully identified (e.g. Martin et al., 2013). Furthermore, the detection of more complex physical behaviours, including housework and other everyday activities, has also been proven feasible in a number of works. Some works have explored the use of these sensors to detect commuting activities and even determine the transportation means by analyzing the natural vibration of the vehicle (Hur et al., 2017). Activity recognition systems based on inertial sensor data are shown to be dependent on the specific location and placement of the sensors. These limitations have been overcome in a number of works by either exploiting the use of location-independent features (e.g. Han et al., 2012, 2014) or identifying in the first place the actual location of the smartphone to use a customized activity identification model.

Cognitive sensing. Cognitive sensing is possibly the most challenging task since there is not a smartphone sensor that can directly measure cognition-related processes. Humans' cognitive functions can be divided into six main categories, including perception, attention, memory, language skills, visuospatial processing and executive functioning, which can be monitored by assessing the performance at specific tasks (Schmidt et al., 2007). Specifically, the attentional system of a user can be evaluated by assessing the user's alertness, which modulates sensory, motor and cognitive processing (van Dongen et al., 2005). Thus, cognitive performance can vary significantly during the day and among different users and can be affected by multiple individual factors, such as the need to sleep at a specific time and based on the body clock, or by user's social obligations.

It is also possible to track user's behaviour and cognitive state by evaluating the screen touch events while using a smartphone device. Specifically, data on screen touches can be used to evaluate the speed and the response time to smartphone surveys in order to track short-term cognitive states, such as attention and alertness (Torous et al., 2016). Additionally, screen touch patterns can be employed to detect quality metrics, sleeping duration and whether the subject uses the phone during nighttime, leading to the monitoring of long-term cognitive states in many mental disorders, such as schizophrenia and depression (Gravenhorst et al., 2015). A recent work has explored the use of the so-called cognitive experience sampling methods, which go beyond traditional clinical questionnaires while introducing a myriad of tasks that users can perform on the phone, ubiquitously and opportunistically, in order to measure the cognitive functioning of the user (Wohlfahrt-Laymann et al., 2018).

Emotional sensing. There is a great number of studies using smartphone technologies for detecting emotional states and mood disorders. The most common way to detect emotional states on a smartphone is based on collecting user's self-reported data through an application, sometimes also including cognitive and physical behavioural states. Smartphone devices can also be used to automatically sample data for the monitoring and treatment of many mental disorders. Specifically, assumptions can be made about the subject's current mood through statistical analysis of some mobile sensing modalities, such as variations in phone usage patterns, texting and calling (Gravenhorst et al., 2015). For instance, an unusual increased number of outgoing phone calls could be related to a change in the mental state of patient (Muaremi et al., 2013). Furthermore, many studies consider audio and voice recognition methods in order to extract user's mood and detect short-term emotional behaviour through sound and phone call features. Examples of phone call features are the number of calls, the number of involved ID phone callers and the sum, average and standard deviation length of calls (Grünerbl et al., 2015). Sound features consist of speech and voice features acquired through phone's microphone including, for example, features related to phone call interaction (e.g. the average speaking length and duration) and audio recordings (detect emotions based on user's voice) (Grünerbl et al., 2015). Vanello et al. (2012) used speech signals to extract voice features related to pitch and pitch changes, combined with acquired ECG signals from external device, in order to characterize the mood of bipolar patients to depressive, hypomanic and euthymic state.

Additionally, other smartphone sensing modalities such as GPS, accelerometer and Wi-Fi signal strength, most frequently used for physical activity sensing, can also provide here valuable information about the patients' state (Gravenhorst et al., 2015). Lomranz et al. (1988) showed that the outdoor behaviour of patients is related to their mental states. Gravenhorst et al. (2015) explained that depressed patients can be isolated into their rooms, spending most of the time in bed, while manic patients tend to travel long distances in an unusual way. Moreover, physical activity levels measured through the smartphone's acceleration sensors and GPS traces have been proved adequate for psychiatric assessment of depression, when long-term data series over a period of days or weeks are considered.

Social sensing. Social networking sites, such as Twitter and Facebook, have been used to study users' social behaviour through computers, smartphones and tablets. Users' actions, posts, comments and sentiments have been examined in order to extract useful information through the Internet regarding not only their mood but also their social activity and interaction with other users (Alp et al., 2018; Xu et al., 2018) Additionally, there is ongoing research on sampling social behaviour data through smartphone devices, especially focussing on the correlation of social inactivity with many mental disorders. Burns et al. (2011) developed a system for patients with depression to detect the user's location and measure the interaction level with friends. They sampled data for emotional and social sensing, using sensors such as accelerometer, GPS, Wi-Fi, Bluetooth and other parameters from phone usage.

Furthermore, Lane et al. (2014) measured social isolation based on the total duration of ambient conversations by using a mobile phone microphone. Moturu et al. (2011) studied Bluetooth proximity detection to estimate the sociability level of people and predict their mood. Mobile devices can also be used to measure long-term behavioural cues and social signals and reveal relevant determinants of health.

In conclusion, this is just a brief overview of the potential of using sensor data in integration with the design of our online experiments, given that participants increasingly use mobile devices to complete them. Adding wearable smart technology, for example, smartphones introduce a further range of sensors and data. A commercially available iWatch 7 includes ECG, heart rate monitor, oxygen levels and more. Physiological measures can be combined with all the different forms of sensing previously described.

5.7 Chapter summary

In this chapter, we have presented and discussed the following topics:

- We have introduced and explained the role of affordance and design issues in online experiments. Affordance is the perceivable actionable properties of objects, and it is considered in the design of visual elements of an online experiment.
- In addition, we reflected on the importance of the role of visual elements such as colours, fonts and modes of presentation. The role of visual design choices in scales, midpoints, spacing of polarities, etc. can affect respondents.
- Next, we discussed the nature and role of metadata and paradata for online experiments. Metadata comprise information collected along with the experiment responses and the actual answers. Paradata are empirical measurements about the process of creating the experiment data; they refer to recordings of the fieldwork process. Paradata can be *directly* recorded – in this case, and we talk of direct paradata. They are an integral part of available software to develop and carry out online experiment. *Indirect paradata* are those collected by adding instruments, for example, eye-tracking devices, skin conductance setups and video recording systems.
- After, we have discussed the practical but essential features of implementation such as length, timing and dynamic stimuli in online experiments. The length of an online experiment interacts with its design and, most notably, with the choice of a between-participants or within-participants design. Moreover, we have learned that visual dynamic stimuli presented on screen

in an online experiment are constrains by the *refresh rate* of screens.

- In this section, we also examined the role of input devices such as the mouse. There are two types of mouse inputs that are useful in online experiments: *mouse clicks and mouse movements*. Mouse clicks are the most straightforward type of input because they can be associated not only with the selection of options in the screen but also with other type of interaction. Mouse movements can be used as proxy of participants' attention and visualized using heat maps.

- The last part of the chapter was devoted introducing a new development in digital social research, the use of sensors from smart devices. Using smart devices like smartphone and smartwatch, we can identify four main types of sensors: *physical sensing, cognitive sensing, emotional sensing* and *social sensing*.

Further readings

There are no specific books on the look and feel of online experiments, but rather similar aspects have been discussed in the context of web surveys. Of this kind, a recommended reading is:

- Tourangeau, Conrad and Couper's *The science of web surveys* (2013), which includes two chapters on the visual elements that are still useful in the context of online experiments, given their nature of a hybrid between online surveys and experiments.

Moving on the issue of metadata and paradata, while both are largely dependent on the platform that a researcher will use, a general complete discussion is:

- Callegaro et al. (2015), *Web Survey Methodology*, which again focusses on web surveys, but conceptual issues are very similar to those of online experiment implementation as we have discussed in this chapter.

Regarding the use of mobile data and sensors, while there are no specific books about their application for social scientific research, there are several texts that complement each other:

- Frith's *Smartphone as Locative Media* (2015), which explains well the potential for location data collected by smartphones for scientific research;
- similar but more technical is the volume by Yang and Yao, *Travel Behavior Characteristics Analysis Technology Based on Mobile Phone Location Data: Methodology and Empirical Research* (2022);
- as part of the Ling et al.'s *Oxford Handbook of Mobile Communication and Society* (2020), a chapter is dedicated to mobile methods.

There are valid resources online about the mobile methods, for example:

- Moles et al.'s (2020) *Mobile Methods* online resources as part of the SAGE research methods platform.

6

DEALING WITH MISSING DATA AND NON-COMPLIANCE

━━━━━━ Chapter objectives ━━━━━━

- To understand the role of attrition and therefore missing data and its effect on the average treatment effect
- To introduce non-parametric methods on missing data
- To understand the notion of compliance using the example of one-sided non-compliance

━━━━━━ Key concepts ━━━━━━

- Attrition is the ratio of the loss of participants during an experiment.
- Missingness is pervasive in studies because researchers rarely manage to gather all of the information that they need from everyone in their sample.
- One-sided non-compliance is a situation when one-sided subjects assigned to the treatment condition do not receive treatment, but all participants assigned to the control condition go untreated.

6.1 Attrition and average treatment effects

In order to facilitate our discussion of attrition and its consequences for estimation, we introduce some new notations. The key idea behind this notation is that 'missingness' is itself a potential outcome – whether the outcome of a subject is reported may depend on the experimental group to which the subject was assigned. For ease of presentation, this section assumes that the assigned treatment (z_i) is identical to the treatment that each subject actually receives (d_i).

For each subject i, we define potential outcomes $Y_i(z)$ for $z \in (0,1)$. Because we assume in this chapter that treatment assigned is the same as treatment received, $z = 0$ when the subject i is not treated and 1 when the subject is treated. When there is no attrition, we observe $Y_i = Y_i(0)(1 - z_i) + Y_i(1)z_i$.

That is, we observe either $Y_i(0)$ or $Y_i(1)$ depending on whether the subject is assigned to the treatment or the control group. Attrition prevents us from measuring Y for some participants. To capture this possibility, we define a new potential outcome, $r_i(z)$, which denotes whether or not the outcome data for subject i are reported when the treatment assignment is z. Let $r_i = 1$ when the outcome is reported, and let $r_i = 0$ when the outcome is missing. Whether participant outcomes are reported or missing may depend on the participants' group assignment. Notice that the non-interference assumption has been applied to attrition: the potential outcomes $r_i(1)$ and $r_i(0)$ depend only on the participants' own treatment assignment. Collecting the notation, the observed reporting outcome r_i is determined by each participant's treatment assignment and potential outcomes:

$$r_1 = r_1(0)(1 - z_i) + r_1(1)z_i \tag{6.1}$$

Attrition occurs when some values of r_i are zero. Because the observed r_i depends on treatment assignment, it is possible for some participants to have the potential for attrition even if no attrition actually occurs. Following the notation convention we used when discussing treatments and treatment assignments, we use lowercase r_i when describing whether subject i reported an outcome in a past experiment and use uppercase R_i to refer to whether subject i reports an outcome in a hypothetical experiment. The expression r_i refers to a fixed quantity, whereas R_i refers to a random variable.

The observed outcomes Y_i require a bit more explanation. The model of missingness presented here presupposes that there is an underlying $Y_i(0)$ or $Y_i(1)$ whose value will either become known to the researcher or not based on whether r_i is 1 or not. Rather than using the complicated notation $Y_i(z, r(z))$ to refer to potential outcomes, we assume that potential outcomes $Y_i(0)$ or $Y_i(1)$ are unaffected by whether these outcomes are reported. Formally, this simplifying assumption amounts to an exclusion restriction: $Y_i(z) = Y_i(z, r(z) = 1) = Y_i(z, r(z) = 0)$. These potential outcomes are translated into observed outcomes according to the following rule:

$$Y_i = Y_i(0) + [Y_i(1) - Y_i(0)]z_i \text{ if } r_i = 1;$$
$$Y_i \text{ is missing if } r_i = 0. \tag{6.2}$$

With this notation in place, let us see how attrition may lead to bias. Recall that the average treatment effect (ATE) is the average difference in the potential outcomes $Y_i(1)$ and $Y_i(0)$ for the entire collection of participants. When the outcomes for the entire treatment and control groups are observed, the treatment group's outcomes are a random sample of $Y_i(1)$ for the pool of participants, and the control group's outcomes are a random sample of $Y_i(0)$ values.

The average outcome in each experimental group provides an unbiased estimate of $\mu_{Y(1)}$ and $\mu_{Y(0)}$. When attrition occurs, the participants for whom we have recorded outcomes may no longer be representative of the subject pool. As a result, the difference in the average of the observed values of $Y_i(1)$ and $Y_i(0)$ will not, in general, produce an unbiased estimate of the ATE.

For example, the expected potential outcome under treatment may be written as a weighted average of outcomes among those who are observable and those who are missing:

$$E[Y_i(1)] = E[R_i(1)]E[E_i(1)|R_i(1) = 1] + \{1 - E[R_i(1)]\}E[Y_i|R_i(1) = 0] \tag{6.3}$$

Similarly, the expected outcome in the control group is

$$E[Y_i(0)] = E[R_i(0)]E[E_i(0)|R_i(0) = 1] + \{1 - E[R_i(0)]\}E[Y_i|R_i(0) = 0] \tag{6.4}$$

Thus, the ATE may be expressed as

$$E[Y_i(1) - Y_i(0) = E[Y_i(1)] = E[R_i(1)]E[E_i(1)|R_i(1) = 1] \\ + \{1 - E[R_i(1)]\}E[Y_i|R_i(1) = 0] - E[Y_i(0) = E[R_i(0)]E[E_i(0)|R_i(0) = 1] \\ + \{1 - E[R_i(0)]\}E[Y_i|R_i(0) = 0]$$

(6.5)

By comparison, the expected difference in potential outcomes when we restrict the average to participants with non-missing values is

$$E[Y_i(1)|(R_i(1) = 1)] = E[Y_i(1)|(R_i(1) = 1)]$$ (6.6)

Comparing Eqs. (6.5) and (6.6), we see that, depending on the relationship between $R_i(z)$ and $Y_i(z)$, the ATE for all participants and the ATE for non-missing participants may be quite different. One special case in which the two quantities are the same arises when the random variables $R_i(z)$ and $Y_i(z)$ are independent. In that case:

$$E[Y_i(1)|R_i(1) = 1] = E[Y_i(1)|R_i(1) = 0]$$ (6.7)

and

$$E[Y_i(0)|R_i(0) = 1] = E[Y_i(0)|R_i(0) = 0]$$ (6.8)

In this special case, Eq. (6.5) simplifies to Eq. (6.6), indicating that when missingness is unrelated to potential outcomes for Y_i, the ATE for the subject pool is identical to the ATE among the non-missing.

6.2 Non-parametric methods for missing data

Most missing data analysis techniques have focussed on using model parameter estimation which depends on modern statistical data analysis methods such as maximum likelihood and multiple imputation. In fact, these modern methods are better than traditional methods (e.g. complete data analysis and mean imputation approaches) and in many particular applications can give unbiased parametric estimation. Because these modern approaches depend on linear parametric regression, they do not give good results, especially if the data distribution has highly non-linear behaviour.

One relatively innocuous form of attrition occurs when data are missing independent of potential outcomes (MIPO). Stated formally, data are MIPO if

$$Y_i(z) \perp R_i(z) \tag{6.9}$$

In other words, this independence condition implies that learning whether a subject's outcomes are potentially missing gives you no clues about the values of $Y_i(1)$ or $Y_i(0)$. Occasionally, this condition is satisfied by the research design itself. For example, survey experiments sometimes divide participants into random subgroups and measure each subgroup's outcomes with a different set of questions. In this case, a random procedure creates missingness, and random missingness implies that $R_i(z)$ is independent of not only potential outcomes but also background attributes. More often, the claim that data are missing independent of outcomes is rooted not in a random procedure but rather an assumption about the unknown process by which some observations are recorded while others go missing.

When data are MIPO, the special conditions of Eqs. (6.7) and (6.8) apply. The ATE among the observed outcomes equals the ATE for the entire sample:

$$E[Y_i(1)|R_i(1) = 1] - E[Y_i(0)|R_i(0) = 1] = E[Y_i(1)] - E[Y_i(0)]. \tag{6.10}$$

Intuitively, if there were no systematic relationship between missingness and potential outcomes, an average of observed outcomes in the treatment group would in expectation equal the average of the $Y_i(1)$ potential outcomes. A parallel argument applies to the control group. As a thought exercise, suppose you have a collection of five measurements. If you adopted the procedure of randomly discarding two of them, would the expected value of the three remaining observations be equal to the average of the five observations? Yes, and this is why the difference-in-means estimator remains an unbiased estimator of the ATE in the presence of random attrition. Although missingness independent of potential outcomes cannot be verified directly, one can gather some circumstantial evidence about its plausibility. This indirect approach starts with a model of random missingness and evaluates its empirical adequacy. If missingness were literally brought about by a random procedure that deleted outcome data, we would expect to find no systematic relationship between r_i and the participants' background attributes or their experimental assignment.

Under some conditions, a simple comparison of observed group averages may be highly informative. If all participants are either never missing outcomes or always missing outcomes, an unweighted comparison of the average treatment and control group outcomes provides an unbiased estimate of the treatment effect for a subset of the participant pool, called *Always-Reporters*: participants who report their outcomes regardless of group assignment. The ATE for this subgroup will not generally be the same as the overall subject pool ATE. We first describe this new estimand and how it is estimated, and then discuss conditions under which this special pattern of attrition might occur.

A special form of attrition occurs when $r_i(1) = r_i(0)$ for all i. In this case, missingness is unaffected by treatment assignment. Suppose we want to estimate the ATE for the subset of participants for whom $r_i(1) = r_i(0) = 1$.

When participants are randomly assigned to control and treatment groups, the expected average of the observed outcomes is $E[Y_i(0)|R_i(0) = 1]$ and $E[Y_i(1)|R_i(1) = 1]$, respectively. Because $r_i(1) = r_i(0)$ for all i, the expected difference between observed treatment and control group averages can be rewritten as $E[(Y_i(1) - Y_i(0))|R_i(0) = R_i(1) = 1]$. In the special case where participants are either Always-Reporters or Never-Reporters, the difference between the treatment and control group averages is an unbiased estimator of the treatment effect for a particular group of participants, Always-Reporters.

In practice, researchers frequently encounter situations where attrition is thought to be related to potential outcomes but not to experimental groups to which participants are assigned. When the outcome variable is an administrative record, it is often reasonable to suppose that participants' group assignments have no effect on whether their outcomes are missing. In voter turnout experiments, some jurisdictions are slow to update their records after the election. All those who live in the affected geography, whether treated or untreated, are missing outcome data and would be missing regardless of treatment assignment. A simple comparison of treatment and control group averages among the remaining participants provides the ATE among those who always have outcome data (those participants from places where administrative records are available).

Another situation in which attrition may be unrelated to treatment assignment occurs when there are delays between the intervention and measurement of the outcome. Outcomes may be missing because participants have moved away. Obtaining an unbiased estimate of the ATE among Always-Reporters can be valuable. First, treatment effect estimates are useful in assessing theoretical predictions about interventions. These predictions may be stated in very general terms, in which case the estimated ATE of any group, including Always-Reporters, may help shed light on whether the prediction holds. Second, the treatment effect among those who always have outcome data may be what the researcher seeks when evaluating an intervention.

When attrition is neither random, random conditional on X, nor confined to, the researcher is forced to fall back on other ways of extracting inferences from the available outcomes. There are two main strategies. First, the researcher may be able to place bounds on the treatment effect, estimating the largest and smallest ATEs that would obtain if the missing information were filled in with extremely high or low outcomes. This cautious approach has the virtue of imposing few assumptions. A second approach is to fashion a statistical model that reflects the specific sources of missingness in a given application. Because these models often invoke strong assumptions about the functional form linking inputs and outputs, the distribution of unobserved variables and homogeneity of treatment effects, the latter approach is in tension with the agnostic style of experimental investigation. For that reason, we focus on the first approach.

Extreme value bounds gauge the potential consequences of attrition by examining how the estimated ATE varies depending on how one fills in missing potential outcomes. To see how this works, suppose that the $Y_i(z)$ measured can range from 0 to 10. It is assumed that 0 and 10 represent the range of possible values for all subject outcomes, missing or not. Suppose we randomly assign the subject pool to treatment and control groups. For example, let participants 2, 3, 5 and 7 be assigned to treatment and 1, 4, 6 and 8 be assigned to control. Had there been no attrition, the average for the treatment group would be $(7 + 10 + 6 + 6)/4 = 29/4 = 7.25$, and the control group average would be $(3 + 7 + 5 + 6)/4 = 21/4 = 5.25$. If all potential outcomes were observed, the estimated treatment effect would be 2. Due to attrition, however, not all the potential outcomes are observed. Instead, we have for the treatment group $(7 + 10 + ? + ?)/4 = ?$ and for the control group $(? + 7 + 5 + 6)/4 = ?$, where question marks denote quantities unknown due to attrition. To find the upper bound on the treatment effect estimate, substitute 10 for the missing values in the treatment group and 0 for the missing value in the control group. The lower bound is formed by filling in the missing values in the treatment group with 0 and the missing value in the control group with 10:

$$\text{Upper bound}: \frac{37}{4} - \frac{18}{4} = \frac{19}{4}$$
$$\text{Lower bound}: \frac{17}{4} - \frac{28}{4} = -\frac{11}{4}$$

First, notice that the upper and lower bounds contain the true ATE of 2. Although the extreme value bounds are in this case sample estimates and therefore subject to sampling variability, extreme value bounds tend to be successful in bracketing the true ATE. Second, the bounds are wide. This is frequently the case with extreme value bounds due to the assumption-free manner in which the bounds are constructed. For experiments with a modest share of missing observations and a narrow range of feasible outcomes, these bounds can be quite useful. As the rate of attrition increases or as the range of possible Y_i values expands, extreme value bounds become less informative. Indeed, extreme value bounds are undefined when Y_i has infinite range. However, bounds can be formed for trans-formations of Y_i when this is the case; redefine the outcome variable to be 1 if Y_i is greater than a certain value and 0 otherwise. By 'coarsening' the data, one obtains extreme value bounds on an ATE that is now defined in terms of a binary outcome.

6.3 One-sided non-compliance

When conducting experiments in natural settings, researchers are sometimes unable to administer the treatment to all participants assigned to the treatment group. Failure-to-treat may occur for a variety of reasons. Logistical snags are common. Treatments plan-ned for a particular area may be scrubbed because of miscommu-nication, staffing shortages or transportation problems. Sometimes participants targeted for treatment prove challenging to reach. For example, voter mobilization experiments that send canvassers to speak with registered voters about an upcoming election often find that a significant fraction of participants are not home when can-vassers arrive. In other experiments, participants may refuse the treatment. An encouragement design invites participants in the assigned treatment group to participate in a programme offered by the researchers. Only some of those invited may elect to participate. Failure-to-treat, in short, means that the assigned treatment group is no longer the same as the group that is treated.

In the vocabulary of experiments, the term *compliance* is used to describe whether the actual treatment coincides with the assigned treatment. Under full compliance, all participants assigned to the treatment group receive the treatment, and no subject assigned to the control group receives the treatment. Non-compliance occurs when participants who were assigned to receive the treatment go untreated or when participants assigned to the control group are treated inadvertently. In everyday language, the compliance and non-compliance of the terms have connotations of agreeableness on the one hand and disobedience on the other. The experimental terminology has no normative connotations. As the face-to-face canvassing example shows, non-compliance may occur without any refusal on the part of the participants.

In this section, we focus on one-sided non-compliance, which occurs when there is non-compliance for only one of the assigned groups. We restrict our focus to the case most relevant for social science applications, which occurs when no subject assigned to the control group is treated but some of those assigned to the treatment group go untreated. A common experimental design that displays one-sided non-compliance is a study in which the treatment is available only through the experiment. There is no opportunity for the control group to be treated without the cooperation of the experimenters.

To appreciate the challenges posed by one-sided non-compliance, suppose that you are interested in assessing the effectiveness of an online canvassing effort on COVID-19 vaccination, which is measured for each subject using public records of who got a jab. Imagine 4,000 participants are randomly divided into two equal groups (2,000 treatment and 2,000 control), and canvassers are sent out to contact the participants in the treatment group. In the familiar case of full compliance, 100% of those assigned to the treatment group receive the treatment. As discussed before, in experiments with full compliance, an unbiased estimate of the average causal effect of the treatment can be calculated by subtracting the average outcome in the control group from the average outcome in the treatment group. However, in online canvassing experiments, not everyone will be found at their listed contact details when the canvassers contact them (some info might be outdated, some might be blocked by spam or other security online features). Typically, only 25% of those assigned to the treatment group can be reached by the canvassers; the remaining 75% of the treatment group goes untreated. Applying these rates to our hypothetical canvassing example, we observe the average outcomes for three groups of participants: the 500 participants assigned to the treatment group who are actually treated, the 1,500 participants assigned to the treatment group who remain untreated and the 2,000 (untreated) participants in the control group.

Now suppose you were the principal investigator of this study. How should the data from these three groups be analyzed? Which causal effects can be estimated using these data?

One option is to ignore the issue of non-compliance and compare the average outcome for the entire treatment group (all 2,000 observations) with the average outcome of the 2,000 subject control group. This comparison is what we examine when analyzing an experiment with full compliance: we subtract the control group average from the treatment group average. But recall that only 25% of the treatment group was treated. If the apparent difference in average group outcomes is interpreted as an ATE for the *entire* group of participants, this method implicitly assumes that the ATE is zero for the untreated portion of the treatment group. To assume that the untreated members of the treatment group have an ATE of zero is to assert that their average outcomes would be no different if they had been treated, which seems implausible. As an alternative to comparing the average outcomes based on which group a subject is assigned to, how about comparing the average outcome among participants in the treatment group who receive the treatment (500 participants) to the average outcome among the control group (2,000 participants)? Despite the intuitive appeal of this approach, there is a serious problem with comparing the *actually* treated to the untreated. The participants who are actually treated are a non-random subset of the original treatment group. This point cannot be emphasized enough. Unlike groups formed by random assignment, groups formed *after* random assignment will not in general have the same expected potential outcomes. Comparing these groups opens the door to biased inference. We need to discuss the problem in formal terms, introducing the idea that the subject pool consists of two groups: participants who will be treated if and only if they are assigned to the treatment group and participants who will never be treated regardless of which group they are assigned to. The upshot of this formal discussion is that experiments with one-sided non-compliance tell us only about the ATE among participants who take the treatment if assigned to be treated. This limitation forces researchers to interpret their results more cautiously. Failure-to-treat also has important implications for experimental design, particularly when researchers have reason to anticipate high rates of non-compliance.

Whether subject i receives the treatment is denoted d_i, where $d_i = 1$ indicates that subject i is treated and $d_i = 0$ indicates that subject i is not treated. For each subject, we define potential outcomes, the set of outcomes that might occur. The outcome measure of greatest interest to the researcher is typically labelled Y_i. The potential outcome $Y(d)$ refers to the outcome that subject i would exhibit when $d_i = d$. Specifically, $Y_i(1)$ is the potential outcome when the subject i is treated, and $Y_i(0)$ is the potential outcome when the subject i is not treated. When writing potential outcomes as $Y_i(d)$ rather than $Y_i(\mathbf{d})$, we are invoking the non-interference assumption. Potential outcomes are written solely in terms of the treatment that subject i receives; treatments received by other participants are assumed to be irrelevant. Assuming non-interference holds, the causal effect of the treatment on a subject i is $Y_i(1) - Y_i(0)$. Recall that the problem of estimating causal effects stems from the fact that we never observe both $Y_i(1)$ and $Y_i(0)$; we observe each subject either in a treated or untreated state. In order to build non-compliance into this modelling framework, we expand the notation to account for the possibility that assigned treatment may not always coincide with the actual treatment. The set of variables that may be influenced by treatment assignment now includes not only the outcome variable Y_i but also whether an individual is treated (d_i).

In order to distinguish assigned treatment from actual treatment, let the experimental assignment of subject i be denoted z_i. When $z_i = 1$, the subject is assigned to the treatment group, and when $z_i = 0$, the subject is assigned to the control group. In previous sections, $d_i = z_i$: all participants assigned to the treatment group are treated, and no participants assigned to the control group are treated. We now relax this constraint and consider actual treatment to be a potential outcome. Let $d_i(z)$ represent whether subject i is actually treated when the treatment assignment is z. For compactness, we write $d_i(z = 1)$ as $d_i(1)$ and $d_i(z = 0)$ as $d_i(0)$. For example, if a subject would be treated if assigned to the treatment group, $d_i(1) = 1$. If a subject would receive no treatment if assigned to the treatment group, $d_i(1) = 0$. For each subject, a pair of potential outcomes, $d_i(1)$ and $d_i(0)$, indicate whether the subject will receive the treatment if assigned to the treatment or control group. For the case of one-sided non-compliance, $d_i(0)$ is set to 0 for all i: participants are never treated when they are assigned to the control group $d_i(1)$; however, they can be either 0 or 1.

Participants in experiments with one-sided non-compliance can be divided into two groups. Participants are called *Compliers* if their potential outcomes meet two conditions: they receive the treatment if assigned to the treatment group ($d_i(1) = 1$), and they do not receive the treatment if assigned to the control group ($d_i(0) = 0$). These participants 'comply' with their treatment assignment inasmuch as they receive the treatment when assigned to the treatment group and do not receive the treatment when assigned to the control group. In contrast, those for whom $d_i(1) = 0$ and $d_i(0) = 0$ are called *Never-Takers*. They never take the treatment regardless of whether they are assigned to the treatment group or control group. Because $d_i(0) = 0$ for all participants, when discussing one-sided non-compliance, researchers sometimes refer to Never-Takers using the shorthand $d_i(1) = 0$ and refer to *Compliers* using the shorthand $d_i(1) = 1$. For example, the expression ATE $| (d_i(1) = 1)$ would be read as the ATE among *Compliers*.

When classifying participants as either *Compliers* or Never-Takers, three points should be kept in mind. First, this terminology has nothing whatsoever to do with outcomes, Y_i. The terms *Compliers* and *Never-Taker* refer only to whether participants would take the treatment if assigned to the treatment group. Second, the definition of d_i given above presupposes an abstract treatment that is either administered or not. When conducting an experiment, a researcher must define the criteria that will be used to classify each subject as treated or untreated. In some cases, the definition of treatment is unambiguous. In a study designed to test the efficacy of a message to promote vaccination, participants are either exposed to it or not. In other cases, formulating a definition is less straightforward. For example, what if the treatment is a yearlong class, but some participants only attend for a few months? The definition of treatment affects the definition of a *Complier*. Finally, the classification of participants as either *Compliers* or *Never-Takers* reflects not only the participants' background attributes but also the experimental context and experimental design. For example, if a face-to-face canvassing effort is conducted only on weekends, a subject who is home every weeknight but gone every weekend will be a *Never-Taker*. If the experimenter instead instructs canvassers to work weeknights but not weekends, this same subject would now be a *Complier*. Each participant's potential outcome $d_i(z)$ depends on how the treatment is administered. For this reason, it is important for researchers to clearly describe their procedures and the context in which the experiment occurred. Otherwise, it will be difficult for readers to get a sense of who the *Compliers* are when interpreting the results.

The first step is to re-examine, in light of the possibility of non-compliance, the two core assumptions: non-interference and excludability.

This assumption consists of two parts. Part A stipulates that whether a subject is treated depends only on the subject's own treatment group assignment. Other participants' assignments are assumed to have no bearing on whether one receives the treatment. In order to depict this assumption formally, define z as a list of treatment assignments for each of the N participants. The treatment assignment of subject i is one of the N elements of this list. Imagine altering the treatment assignments of some or all of the other participants while keeping the treatment assignment of subject i the same. Call any such altered list of assignments z' Part A of the non-interference assumption states that

$$d_i(z) = d_i(z') \text{ if } z = z' \tag{6.11}$$

where the notation $z_i = z_i'$ means that subject i keeps the same treatment assignment even when the assignments of other participants change. Part B says that the potential outcomes are affected by (1) the subject's own assignment and (2) the treatment that the subject receives as a consequence of that assignment. Other participants' assignments and treatments are assumed to have no bearing on one's outcomes.

$$Y_i(z,d) = Y_i(z',d') \text{ if } z_i = z_i' \text{ and } d_i = d_i' \tag{6.12}$$

The plausibility of the non-interference assumption depends on the specifics of a given experiment. The rule of thumb when assessing the validity of this assumption is to reflect on whether potential outcomes vary depending on how participants are allocated to experimental groups or how treatments are actually administered. Imagine once more a canvassing experiment in which two of the participants live on remote locations, and suppose that if one remote location participant is assigned to the treatment group, canvassers will be tired to travel to the participant's house in other remote location. Regardless of whether the first remote location participant is treated, Part A of the non-interference assumption is violated because one subject's assignment affects whether the other subject receives the treatment. Part B would be violated if one participant's potential outcomes are affected by other participants' assigned or actual treatments. Non-interference would be violated if, as a consequence of being canvassed, treated participants tell their neighbours about the upcoming election, changing these participants' propensity to vote. Assuming non-interference greatly simplifies the schedule of potential outcomes, allowing us to write them solely in terms of the treatment that subject i is assigned or receives. We next distinguish the causal effect of treatment assignment from the causal effect of receiving the treatment. The causal effect of assignment to the treatment group is called the *intent-to-treat* effect because it reflects the intended assignments, not the actual treatments. The intent-to-treat effect can be defined for any set of potential outcome that may be affected by treatment assignment, such as $d_i(z)$, $Y_i(d(z))$ or $Y_i(z, d(z))$. The intent-to-treat effect of z on d for each participant is defined as:

$$\text{ITT}_{i,D} \equiv d_i(1) - d_i(0) \tag{6.13}$$

When we calculate the average $\text{ITT}_{i,D}$ across all participants, we obtain ITT_D, which is the proportion of participants who are treated in the event that they are assigned to the treatment group minus the proportion who would have been treated even if they had instead been assigned to the control group:

$$\text{ITT}_D \equiv E\left[\text{ITT}_{i,D}\right] = E[d_i(1)] - E[d_i(0)] \tag{6.14}$$

Since we are assuming one-sided non-compliance, $E[d_i(0)] = 0$, and the expression ITT_D simplifies to $E[d_i(1)]$.

The intent-to-treat effect of z_i on Y_i for each participant is defined as

$$\text{ITT}_{i,Y} \equiv Y_i(z = 1, d(1)) - Y_i(z = 0, d(0)) \tag{6.15}$$

In the latter way of expressing the $\text{ITT}_{i,Y}$ makes explicit the fact that outcomes may respond to treatment assignment or to the treatments that result from treatment assignment. The average $\text{ITT}_{i,Y}$ is the change in expected potential outcomes that occurs when participants move from an assigned control group ($z = 0$) to an assigned treatment group ($z = 1$):

$$\text{ITT}_Y \equiv \frac{1}{N}\sum_{i=1}^{N}(Y_i(z = 1, d(1)) - Y_i(z = 0, d(0))) = E[Y_i(z = 1, d(1))]$$
$$- E[Y_i(z = 0, d(0))] = E\left[\text{ITT}_{i, Y}\right]. \tag{6.16}$$

For experiments with 100% compliance, treatment assignment is the same as treatment status, and so the ITT_Y is the same as the ATE. Since the average intent-to-treat effect on Y_i is by far the more important of the two intent-to-treat effects, we will drop the subscript and simply call it by the shorthand ITT. The ITT is a measure of the average effect of experimental assignment on outcomes, regardless of the fraction of the treatment group that is actually treated. It is commonly used to describe the effectiveness of a program when the main concern is the extent to which the program changed outcomes. If all you care about is whether the *programme* 'made a difference', non-compliance is in some sense irrelevant. Regardless of whether the programme treated a large or small proportion of its intended targets, did it change the average outcome?

Often, however, researchers seek to estimate the ATE, not the average effect of assignment to treatment. In other words, they want to know the average effect of d_i on Y_i, not the average effect of z_i on

Y_i. The expanded notation for writing potential outcomes allows $Y_i(z, d(z))$ to respond to two inputs: the assigned treatment (z) and the treatment that results from assignment $(d_i(z))$. To isolate the effect of the treatment from the effect of assignment, we extend the excludability.

The excludability assumption stipulates that potential outcomes respond to treatments, not treatment assignments. If we assume non-interference, the excludability assumption may be stated with reference to the treatment that subject i is assigned and receives. For all participants, values of z and values of d,

$$Y_i(z, d) = Y_i(d) \tag{6.17}$$

Untreated participants have the same potential outcomes regardless of their assignments: $Y_i(z = 0, d = 0) = Y_i(z = 1, d = 0)$. The same goes for participants who receive the treatment: $Y_i(z = 0, d = 1) = Y_i(z = 1, d = 1)$. Under the excludability assumption, only d matters; we therefore write the potential outcomes according to whether the subject received the treatment or disregard the assigned treatment. This assumption is called *excludability* or the *exclusion restriction* because it maintains that experimental assignment (z) may be 'excluded' as a cause of Y_i since it has no influence on potential outcomes except insofar as it affects treatment (d). For example, if the exclusion restriction holds, Never-Takers' Y_i. are the same regardless of whether they are assigned to the treatment or control group. For Never-Takers, treatment assignment always results in $d = 0$, and the assignment (z) has no opportunity to affect outcomes. The plausibility of the exclusion restriction must be assessed based on a close inspection of each experiment. The researchers' definition of what constitutes the treatment often points to possible violations of the exclusion restriction. Consider an experiment in which only participants in the treatment group get a letter inviting them to participate in a new programme, and d_i is whether the subject actually participates in the programme. The exclusion restriction states that the letter has no effect on potential outcomes other than through the subject's participation in the programme. Among those who participate in the programme, it is assumed that $Y_i(z = 0, d = 1) = Y_i(z = 1, d = 1)$. Among those who do not participate, it is assumed that $Y_i(z = 0, d = 0) = Y_i(z = 1, d = 0)$. Whether these assumptions are credible depends on one's intuitions about the recruitment letter – does it seem plausible that the letter affects outcomes apart from affecting whether participants participate in the programme? The experiment, as implemented, cannot speak to this issue because everyone in the treatment group received the letter. If this possible violation of the exclusion restriction is taken to be a serious challenge to the claim that participation per se affects results, it may be necessary to conduct a new experiment in which recruitment is encouraged in some other way. For example, a recruitment letter could be sent to both the treatment and control groups, but with the treatment group encouraged to participate sooner. Exclusion restrictions sometimes provoke controversy when researchers implement multifaceted interventions but interpret the experiment as though it reveals the effect of one component of the intervention. To see how this interpretation may lead to a violation of the exclusion restriction, let us again consider an experiment in which eligible voters are encouraged to participate in an upcoming election. Canvassers are sent to the homes of those in the treatment group. If the targeted voter answers the door, the canvasser gives a brief speech about the importance of voting and hands the subject a leaflet that indicates where and when to vote. If no one answers, the leaflet is slipped under the door. If the researcher interprets the study as an investigation of the effects of the verbal message delivered by the canvassers, then the participants who answer the door are considered $d_i(1) = 1$. The exclusion restriction implies that $Y_i(z = 0, d = 0) = Y_i(z = 1, d = 0)$ and that $Y_i(z = 0, d = 1) = Y_i(z = 1, d = 1)$; the subject is assumed to be affected by the speech but not by the leaflet (or any other aspect of treatment assignment). Notice that this complication arises even when *all* participants are treated when assigned to the treatment group. The important implication of this example is that when the experiment involves compound treatments, the researcher must make a choice. Either the definition of the treatment must be adjusted to include the entire package of interventions (leafleting, sometimes in conjunction with a speech) or the researcher must be prepared to stipulate the effect of certain components, such as leafleting. A design implication is that if researchers seek to estimate the distinct effects of each component, they may need to perform a more complex experiment in which different treatment groups receive different interventions. One experimental condition might provide canvassing and leaflets, while another experimental condition might provide only canvassing.

6.3.1 Average treatment effect and complier average casual effects

Non-compliance represents an obstacle to what researchers can understand from an experiment. Normally, we would aim to estimate the ATE as

$$\text{ATE} \equiv \frac{1}{N} \sum_{i=1}^{N} (Y_i(1) - Y_i(0)) = E[Y_i(d = 1) - Y_i(d = 0)] \tag{6.18}$$

However, when we have non-compliance in an experiment, we do not generate the information needed to estimation of the ATE. In this scenario, the goal becomes the estimation of the complier average causal effect (CACE), which is defined as

$$\text{CACE} \equiv \frac{\sum_{i=1}^{N} (Y_i(1) - Y_i(0))d_i(1)}{\sum_{i=1}^{N} d_i(1)} = E[(Y_i(d = 1) - Y_i(d = 0))|d_i(1) = 1]$$

$$\tag{6.19}$$

The CACE is nothing else that the average treatment affect for a subset of the participants that we have labelled as Compliers.

In the previous sections, we discussed the need to calculate ITT, which is the average difference in $Y_i(d(1)) - Y_i(d(0))$ when participants are assigned to the treatment group versus the control group. To calculate the ITT, calculate the difference in Y_i when a subject is assigned to the treatment versus the control group subject by subject, sum these differences and divide by the number of participants. The calculation of the ITT is not affected by the treatment effects among participants who are labelled as Never-Takers (individuals for whom $d_i(1) = 0$ and $d_i(0) = 0$, they are untreated regardless of whether they are assigned to treatment or control). The ITT compares outcomes when participants are assigned to treatment rather than control. Regardless of their assigned condition, Never-Takers are never treated and always exhibit their untreated potential outcomes. An experiment with one-sided non-compliance enables the researcher to estimate the average effect of assignment to treatment (the ITT) and the ATE for a subset of the participants' pool. This subset consists of Compliers, those participants who would be treated if assigned to the treatment group. Whether a participant is a Complier or a Never-Taker is in part a function of the experimental design and the context in which the experiment is conducted. An experimenter can alter the share of Compliers by providing incentives, making the treatment more appealing or working harder to contact participants assigned to the treatment group.

6.3.2 Estimating treatment effects and partial treatment

In some experiments, it is possible for participants to be partially treated. If the treatment is viewing five-part YouTube videos, some participants will decline to participate, others will complete the full programme and some will watch only some of the episodes. If the treatment is exposure to a canvasser's voter mobilization message, participants might slam the door after hearing only part of the intended message. How does partial treatment alter our analysis and interpretation of experiments with non-compliance? If participants are assigned to either treatment or control groups (no participants are assigned to a partial treatment group), it will not be possible to empirically distinguish the average causal effect of partial treatment from the average causal effect of full treatment. Imagine, for example, we were to divide the subject population into three groups: *Compliers, Partial Compliers and Never-Takers*. We can estimate the distribution of types in the subject pool by looking at the results of our attempt to treat the assigned treatment group. The problem, however, is that the control group's outcomes are a weighted average of the three types' untreated potential outcomes. With just two randomly assigned groups, we cannot isolate the contribution of each of the three types. As discussed in the exercises, to identify the effect of partial treatment, we need an augmented experimental design that varies whether participants are encouraged to receive partial or full treatment. Suppose, however, that our experimental design merely assigns participants to treatment and control conditions. Some of the participants assigned to the treatment condition receive full treatment, and others partial treatment. One approach is to define $d = 1$ as full treatment but to err on the side of underestimating the CACE. To implement this approach, the researcher simply considers all partially treated participants as fully treated. Ordinarily, one would assume that the effect of partial treatment is smaller than the effect of full treatment. The estimated CACE moves toward zero under this definition of treatment: the ITT is unaffected by the definition of treatment, but the ITT_D increases when the definition of compliance becomes more permissive. An approach similar in spirit is to bound the CACE by alternative classifications for the partially treated. The lower bound is obtained by classifying the partially treated as treated, and the upper bound is obtained by classifying the partially treated as untreated. The resulting estimates bound the true CACE for full treatment if we assume that the ATE for the partially treated lies between zero and the CACE. Notice that classifying the partially treated as untreated leads to a violation of the exclusion restriction when partial treatment affects outcomes. In this case, the partial treatment affects the ITT, but because the partially treated are classified as untreated, partial treatment will not affect the estimate of ITT_D. If we assume that the ATE of partial treatment is the same sign as the CACE, the absolute size of the treatment effect will be exaggerated by classifying the partially treated as not treated. The magnitude of this bias increases with the size of the treatment effect from partial treatment and the share of participants partially treated.

6.3.3 Final considerations about non-compliance

In conclusion, when conducting experiments in settings where non-compliance is a potential concern, researchers should consider some of the following design recommendations:

1 Conduct a small pilot study in order to see whether non-compliance problems arise and, if so, whether these problems can be overcome by adjusting the treatment or the manner in which it is delivered. If compliance rates are expected to remain low, consider the feasibility of a placebo design.

2 It is better to avoid targeting an excessive number of subjects for treatment. When collaborating with an organization that is enthusiastic about the intervention, researchers are sometimes urged to allocate more participants to the treatment group than the organization can realistically treat. This arrangement sometimes leads to failure-to-treat not because participants failed to cooperate, but because the organization could not deliver the assigned treatments.

3 It is helpful to define the treatment and the criteria used to classify participants as treated or untreated (or partially treated). Ensure that systematic procedures are in place to measure the actual receipt of treatment. Unless you ascertain the proportion of the assigned treatment group that actually receives the treatment, you will not be able to calculate the ITT_D or the CACE.

Each of these approaches requires careful management, supervision and often negotiation, but these timely adjustments in design can make an experiment vastly more informative.

In this section, we explained how to analyze experiments that fail to treat all of the subjects assigned to the treatment group. This type of non-compliance is labelled 'one-sided' because assigned and actual treatment differ in one direction only: some subjects assigned to the treatment condition do not receive treatment, but all participants assigned to the control condition go untreated. Experiments with one-sided non-compliance allow us to estimate the average causal effect among Compliers, not the average causal effect among the entire subject pool. This type of experiment cannot estimate the ATE among Never-Takers because we never observe them in their treated state. The proper way to estimate the CACE is to compare participants assigned to the treatment and control conditions; one should not compare participants who actually receive the treatment to participants who go untreated. Groups formed by random assignment have comparable potential outcomes; groups formed after random assignment often do not.

Readers should be aware that besides one-sided non-compliance, also two-sided one is possible. *Two-sided non-compliance* occurs when some subjects assigned to the control group receive treatment, and some subjects assigned to the treatment group go untreated. To fully discuss two-sided non-compliance is beyond the scope of this book because this form of non-compliance is much more common in field experiments that in the lab or online ones.

6.4 Chapter summary

In this chapter, we have discussed the following issues:

- We discussed attrition's role and missing data and its effect on the ATE. Attrition is the ratio of the loss of participants during an experiment. Missingness is pervasive in studies because researchers rarely gather all the information they need from everyone in their sample. Therefore, attrition can lead to biased estimates in our analysis. Therefore, we discussed how to estimate the ATE considering the case of non-compliance.
- We discussed the notion of compliance and ATE using the example of one-sided non-compliance. One-sided non-compliance is when one-sided subjects assigned to the treatment condition do not receive treatment, but all participants assigned to the control condition go untreated. To achieve that, we divided the subjects population into three groups: *Compliers, Partial Compliers and Never-Takers*.
- In the last part of the chapter, we identified the following steps as a good practices to avoid non-compliance. First, conduct a small

pilot study to see whether non-compliance problems arise and, if so, whether these problems can be overcome by adjusting the treatment or how it is delivered. If compliance rates are expected to remain low, consider the feasibility of a placebo design. Second, it is better to avoid targeting an excessive number of subjects for treatment. When collaborating with an organization that is enthusiastic about the intervention, researchers are sometimes urged to allocate more participants to the treatment group than the organization can realistically treat. This arrangement sometimes leads to failure-to-treat not because participants failed to cooperate but because the organization could not deliver the assigned treatments. Third, defining the treatment and the criteria used to classify participants as treated or untreated (or partially treated) is helpful.

Further readings

Texts concerning the topic treated in this chapter are highly technical. One of the best is Taback's *Design and Analysis of Experiments and Observational Studies Using R* (2022). This book is essentially an advanced introduction to experimental design both in terms of statistics and R programming.

Very similar is Lawson's *Design and Analysis of Experiments with R* (2015); it contains a bit more discussion of incomplete design compared to Taback's one.

Less technical but still very useful is Barak et al.'s *Experimental Designs* (2022). Another interesting book is by Dean et al., *Design and Analysis of Experiments* (2017), which discusses also the experiments carried out in computer science; differences and commonalities are useful to study as the influence of computer science methods in social science has increased.

7

EXECUTION OF POPULATION-BASED SURVEY EXPERIMENTS: CASE STUDIES

━━━━━━━ Chapter objectives ━━━━━━━━━━━━━━━━━━━━━━━━━━

- To introduce the reader to the different possible implementations of online experiments
- To highlight the specific features of one experimental design over another
- To offer a set of examples of online experiments implemented in real studies

━━━━━━━ Key concepts ━━━━━━━━━━━━

- The logic of choice experiments and their implementation online. Discrete choice experiment (DCE) is an attribute-based survey method for measuring benefits (utility). DCEs present respondents

(Continued)

with samples of hypothetical scenarios (choice sets) extracted a priori from all possible choice sets according to statistical design principles.

- What are the main features of vignette studies, and how they can be conducted online? In the contrastive vignette technique approach, researchers examine the ways in which vignette structure influences responses. In its simplest form, it randomly presents minimally contrastive versions of a single vignette (story) to respondents. The minimal contrasts allow experimenters to investigate how the manipulation of a single factor influences respondents' judgements.

- Our choices are influenced by how options are framed through different wordings, reference points and emphasis. A simple and typical framing experiment has participants first provide information about themselves and after are randomly assigned to three different groups as prescribed by a between-participants design. Framing experiments online can be easily executed without the need for specific platforms, which might be the case for experiments that require ad hoc programming, like in the case of the Implicit Association Test or DCE ones.

- Serious games aimed at changing attitudes or behaviours are called *Behaviour Change Games* or *BCGs*. BCGs form a subset of serious games, which were designed in order to support attitude and change behaviours.

- Game features can be categorized into mechanics and components. Game design features are relevant to mechanics, for example, challenges, feedback and rewards, and components, for example, achievements, avatars, badges, leaderboards, levels, points and social graphs, as well as latent game design features.

In this section, we will discuss some examples of online experiments; they all have their specific strengths and weaknesses, some are better suited for some research questions while others are for other. In fact, a common question that is posed by those who would like to design an online experiment is 'What is the best design'? or 'What is a good experiment'? To answer these questions, one should know the details of the research goals and hypothesis of the researcher, the availability of resources that she or he has and the existing literature on the subject. Rather than selecting one overall best design or form of experiment, what we can discuss are some steps to increase the chance that we will come up with a good design. Let us describe some fundamental steps:

1   It is not surprising that the first step should be an accurate literature review. Such a review should include an assessment of the strengths and weaknesses of different experimental designs. An overview of what has worked in the past, if previous studies are comparable to what we want to do, is a good start. At the same time, the review not only serves the purpose of identifying gaps in the existing knowledge but also helps to identify improvements on the shortcomings and limitations of previous studies from the methodological point of view. The literature review will also help in terms of measurement. The non-trivial choice of how to measure the object of interest is one of the crucial decisions, and knowledge of what has been used before is essential in making a good choice.

2   Step 1 will help with the definition of step 2, which consists in identifying the theoretical framework and hypothesis of our study. This part, when conducting empirical work, includes the precise specification of predictors and moderators. Moreover, if we aim to make comparisons, for example, between different treatments, we need to think carefully about how such comparisons will be unbiased.

3   The third step concerns the research design of our study. The first point is to evaluate the source of data, and in an experimental setting, it means the target population and its samples. The other crucial point at this step, we mentioned already in the context of the literature review, is the definition of our experiment measures. These need to be clearly connected to the hypotheses and the theoretical framework in order to maximize construct validity. At this stage, we should be concerned also with issue accuracy if previous experiments help us in defining our power analysis and expectations about effect sizes.

4 The fourth step is a continuation of the previous one about research design. The assessment of the experimental design is often the result of a compromise between complexity and costs and internal and external validity (of our design). Sometimes, a design that addresses all our concerns might be too complex from the implementation point of view. The more complex a design, the higher the number of aspects of the data collection that can go wrong. At this stage, it is useful to develop what is called a *high-level experimental workflow document.* It is often a diagram that shows all the aspects of the design without entering the minute details, but it provides an overview of the level of complexity of a design, see Figure 7.1 as an example drawn from a real study. This document can be also very useful if we

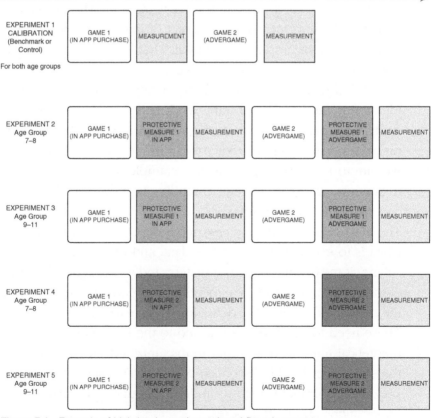

Figure 7.1 Example of high-level experimental workflow document

are working in a team with programmers, in case we need to customize the online platform to collect our experimental data. For example, it can explain the stimuli order and the elements of randomization that are necessary in the design.

5 The fifth step concerns the use of pretests, stimuli and wording of questions if present. This is the part in which a researcher, hopefully not alone, will have to go through all the details of the experiment implementation. In the online context, this usually means two separate aspects. The first one is the selection of the stimuli and choices about their presentation on screen. The second one is controlling the platform or relative code works as planned in terms of presentation of the stimuli and randomization at all levels. This part is usually long and complex but is an essential quality control check.

6 The next step, once we have a design, is to write a data analysis plan. This will be our intended analytical strategy for how the data will be used to test our hypotheses. In the context of an experiment, it translates into detailing the envisaged statistical analysis. At this stage, it is also useful to distinguish, if relevant, between confirmatory and exploratory hypotheses. This document will be necessary for two formal steps that we will see later, but it also gives a chance to review all the statistical assumptions that we might have embedded in the design both explicitly (see optimality designs discussed previously) and implicitly.

7 The seventh step is presenting our experimental protocol to the institutional review board. The board, which can have different names according to the university system in which we do research, has to assess and approve our study in terms of ethics and privacy. The aspects of consent, deception and data protection that we have discussed in Chapter 3 will be the object of evaluation by the members of the board. This process can take a considerable amount of time, and therefore, it is highly recommended to account for it in our plan to deploy our experiment online.

8 The eighth step is about the pre-registration for our experiment. Pre-registration means that we are specifying our research plan

in advance of its deployment, and we are making this plan publicly available in the registry/repository. In the growing expectations about open science, it is a highly recommended step that should be easy to do if the previous steps were followed. In addition, pre-registration separates hypothesis-generating (exploratory) from hypothesis-testing (confirmatory) research. Both are important. But the same data cannot be used to generate and test a hypothesis, which can happen unintentionally and reduce the credibility of your results. Addressing this problem through planning improves the quality and transparency of your research. This helps you clearly report your study and helps others who may wish to build on it.

9 Once we have a protocol, it has been approved by our institutional board, and it has been pre-registered. We have the step of implementation, which is similar to step 5. We test that all stimuli are presented correctly, randomization works fine and data are registered and stored correctly. If we use an existing platform for online experiments or software to develop it (e.g. PsychoPy, OTree), this task is a bit easier. If we have developed our own platform, this step requires extra caution.

10 The last step is to launch the experiment. This is normally done with a 'soft launch', similar to a web survey when we invite a small sub-sample of our participants to complete the experiment to test that everything works as planned. If the experiment works fine, we can scale it up to the full sample. It is important to monitor the completion of the online experiment in the first days to spot potential problems related to the correct functionating of the platform. Bugs can appear, and servers can crash or become very slow. It pays off to monitor the responses for a few days during the data collection.

These ten steps to designing a good experiment can be applied to all types of online experiments. At the same time, there are specific challenges in each typology of experimental methods for the social sciences. In the next sections, we will discuss some examples of online experiments that have different designs and goals. These can be considered as experiments to run separately but, in some cases, can be combined. For example, framing experiments can be combined with choice ones. In fact, very complex studies can adopt a nested design, and several experiments are run simultaneously.

7.1 Decision-making: choice experiments

An example of online experiments that can be operationalized in the context of a questionnaire-like structure is the so-called *choice experiments*. The advantage of these experiments is that they not only collect data on the self-reported preferences of the participants but also contain data on the choices individuals make when confronted with a sequence of choices.

Discrete choice experiments (DCEs) – a quantitative method for assessing the various factors that influence people's choices – has recently emerged as a very attractive method for researchers and policymakers because it provides quantitative information on the relative importance of various characteristics that influence people's choices, as well as the trade-offs between these factors and the likelihood of taking a particular option. This method goes beyond traditional qualitative assessments and provides quantifiable data that can better guide the choice of the most appropriate intervention strategies. It also goes beyond traditional ranking and evaluation exercises that do not provide information on the strength of preference, trade-offs or likelihood of taking. The DCE is an attribute-based survey method for measuring benefits (utility). DCEs present respondents with samples of hypothetical scenarios (choice sets) extracted a priori from all possible choice sets according to statistical design principles. Choice sets comprise two or more alternatives, varying along different characteristics or attributes of interest, and individuals are asked to choose an alternative. More commonly, each respondent faces several choice questions within a single survey.

Let us take a look at what this type of experiment consists of from a technical and statistical point of view. The parameter estimates are standard logit, so the regression coefficients represent the change in the logit for each unit change in the predictor. However, unlike traditional conjoint analysis, which is based on conjoint measurement, which is not a behavioural (choice) theory, DCEs are based on a long-standing and well-tested theory of choice behaviour which can take into account interconnected behaviours. The theory was proposed by Thurstone (1927) and is called *random utility theory* (RUT). Recent work in DCE theory and methods relies heavily on the work of McFadden, who extended Thurstone's original theory of pairwise comparisons (pairs of choice alternatives) to multiple comparisons (e.g. McFadden, 1986; McFadden and Train, 2000; McFadden, 1974; Thurstone, 1927). Unlike conjoint measurement (CM), RUT provides an explanation of the choice behaviour of humans, not numbers.

Specifically, the RUT proposes that there is a latent construct called *utility* in a person's head that cannot be observed by researchers. That is, a person has a 'utility' for each choice alternative, but these utilities cannot be 'seen' by researchers, which is why they are termed *latent*. RUT assumes that latent utilities can be summarized by two components, a systematic (explainable) component and a random (unexplainable) component. Systematic components include attributes that explain differences in choice alternatives and covariates that explain differences in individuals' choices. Random components include all unidentified factors that influence choices. Psychologists further assume that individuals are imperfect measuring devices; thus, random components may also include factors that reflect variability and differences in choices associated with individuals and not the choice options themselves. More formally, the basic axiom of RUT is

$$U_{in} = V_{in} + \epsilon_{in},$$

where U_{in} is the latent and unobservable utility that individual n associates with choice alternative i, V_{in} is the systematic and explainable component of utility that individual n associates with alternative i and in is the random component associated with individual n and option i. According to researchers since there is a random component, utilities (or 'preferences') are inherently stochastic. Thus, researchers can predict the probability that individual

n will choose alternative i, but not the exact alternative that individual n will choose.

Choice experiments are useful in identifying implicit preferences that are difficult to expose a person to when considering multi-dimensional choice situations. They can be combined with experimental treatments and then used to see how framing or anchoring a problem can change the relative importance people give to attributes that characterize choice options. For one example, we used this method in the context of online shopping choices. The objective of the experiments was to test whether greater transparency in the presentation of online search information, details of contractual entities and implications for consumer protection and user reviews and ratings would influence consumer choice. The results show that greater online transparency increases the likelihood of product choice but only under certain conditions. A comparison between the four countries found that the similarities in responses to online transparency were much greater than the differences (Veltri et al., 2023).

An example of a discrete choice online experiment is a recent study (Veltri et al., 2023b) on COVID-19 risk perception. In this online DCE, participants were asked to assess two scenarios in terms of the COVID-19 infection risk, each of them posed. Hence, our DCE aimed at understanding the relative importance of attributes defining the scenarios of contagion. In this study, participants were presented with eight choice sets for a total of 16 scenarios visualized in pairs. In each choice set, they were asked to determine which of the two scenarios posed the highest risk of contagion. Each choice set was constituted by two options, and each option was a combination of the following attributes and their values: (a) people wearing face masks (Yes/No); (b) the duration of the meeting (15 min/90 min); (c) the location of the meeting (indoors/outdoors); (d) the number of people present at the meeting (2 people/10 people) and (e) distance between people (1 metre /2 metres). Figure 7.2 presents an example of a DCE online work; two choices are presented on the participants' screen.

Furthermore, we will discuss the heterogeneity of attributes' importance conditional to several covariates: participants' country, their gender and their age (see section 9.2 about it). One additional

Which of the two situations presented here puts you at a higher risk of being infected by the COVID 19 virus? **CHOOSE ONE (Click on the box or button below the box)**

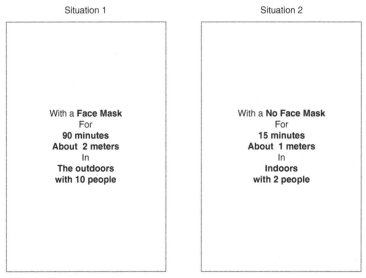

Situation 1

Situation 2

With a **Face Mask**
For
90 minutes
About 2 meters
In
The outdoors
with 10 people

With a **No Face Mask**
For
15 minutes
About 1 meters
In
Indoors
with 2 people

Figure 7.2 Schematic example of the choice cards: in bold the attributes that varied

segmentation explored the use of their cognitive reflection test (CRT) score and their perceived level of fright of COVID-19. The CRT score is computed to identify people with high to low reflective tendency and people with high to low intuitive tendency (Toplak et al., 2014).

The family of choice experiments is very large, and discrete choice ones are only one instance of them. Here are other examples of choice models that can be equally implemented online:

• *Best–worst DCEs (BWDCEs)* are designed to do just that by asking respondents to choose not only the best option in each choice set but also the worst option, followed by the best from the remaining options and so on until an implied preference ordering of the options is obtained. BWDCEs are highly relevant to social science research and are likely to prove useful where DCEs are currently used since they provide richer information on relative preferences between alternatives and significantly larger amounts of choice data, which typically results in gains in statistical efficiency, as we later show. BWDCEs also can help achieve a given target number of choice observations while reducing sample sizes and should prove particularly useful in applications with small sample sizes, arising from budget constraints or small populations from which to sample.

- *Random regret minimization (RRM)*. The fundamental assumption in regret theory is that what matters is not only the realized outcome but also what could have been obtained by selecting a different course of action. This means that the model incorporates anticipated feelings of regret that would be experienced once ex-post decision outcomes are revealed to be 'unfavourable'. The value of an alternative can thus only be assigned following a cross-wise evaluation of alternatives, and this is the cause for substantial increases in computational complexity with large choice sets.

- *Decision field theory (DFT)* originates in mathematical psychology (Busemeyer and Townsend, 1992, 1993) and is very different to both random utility models and RRM. The key assumption under a DFT model is that the preferences for alternatives update over time. The decision-maker considers the alternatives until they reach an internal threshold (similar to the concept of satisficing, where one of the options is deemed 'good enough') or some external threshold (i.e. some time constraint, where a decision-maker stops deliberating on the alternatives as a result of running out of time to make the decision).

Online choice experiments represent a welcome reiteration of a family of experiments with a long history of development in design aspects and the analytical methods applied to them. The idea of conducting choice experiments using smart devices that can provide the previously discussed set of metadata and paradata that can function as covariates in our choice modelling is an intriguing possibility for the future.

7.2 Vignette studies

Behavioural researchers interested in a wide variety of applications have used vignettes or stated choice methods to understand the basis for complex judgements (Louviere et al., 2000). In making decisions, people rarely use a systematic, rational planning process to identify pertinent goals, establish priorities, and weigh evidence on the extent to which various options are likely to enable them to maximize their objectives. More often, people make judgements quickly with limited insights about how they were influenced by the information available to them. Vignettes are among the techniques used by social and behavioural scientists to understand the basis for human judgements on complex issues. The premise of the use of vignettes in surveys is that responses to hypothetical choices provide insights into behaviour in real-world choice situations. A further premise is that hypothetical choices may be informative in ways that are different from and more revealing than respondent opinions about abstract principles. Vignette methods are often used when it is not practical or feasible to study actual behaviour. Vignettes in surveys represent an inexpensive technique for approximating the use of experiments to study behaviour.

Social scientists have long recognized that the narrative mode of thought – storytelling – has advantages for research. Giving respondents a story that features ordinary people, facing a choice, weighing up the pros and cons and making a decision has two significant benefits. First, it engages the interest of respondents; they can identify with the people's dilemma. Second, it gives respondents much more time to think about the issue compared to a standard survey question. These advantages have led to the design of contrastive vignette experiments in social and political science and consumer behaviour. Essentially, the contrastive vignette technique (CVT) combines the causal analysis of experimentation with the power of survey research. Online vignette experiments are increasingly popular because presenting the stories online is much simpler than previous forms of elicitation like face-to-face or telephone interviews.

A first distinction is between two types of vignettes used in surveys: constant variable value vignettes (CVVV) and CVT. When the CVVV approach is used, all research participants are asked to respond to identical vignette content. When CVT methods are used, the vignette structure is systematically varied so that research participants are asked to respond to somewhat different vignette content. In the CVT approach, researchers examine the ways in which vignette structure influences responses. Studies that use the CVVV approach are easier to design and administer than those using CVT methods. However, studies employing CVT methods offer analytic possibilities that far exceed what is possible with data collected with CVVV methods.

In its simplest form, it involves randomly presenting minimally contrastive versions of a single vignette (story) to respondents. The minimal contrasts allow experimenters to investigate how the manipulation of a single factor influences respondents' judgements. In a typical study, each respondent is asked to read one of a number of vignettes and then to answer a set of questions (i.e. dependent variables). Then using multiple regression, the analysis of responses provides a relative weight (level of importance) of the experimental contrasts. To ensure adequate statistical power, a minimum of 100 respondents for each vignette are required. As with experimental designs, three general types of vignette experiments can be distinguished: (a) within-participants designs, (b) mixed designs and (c) between-participants designs. In within-participants designs, each respondent judges exactly the same set of vignettes. The vignette set may either represent the total vignette population, if it is small enough, or a subset of a larger vignette population. In mixed designs, different groups of respondents get different vignette sets, but within each group each respondent receives the same vignettes for judgement. In between-participants designs, each respondent judges only one single vignette, but they are quite rare since serious measurement problems arise, due to different vignette contexts.

A quantitative vignette study consists of two components: (a) a vignette experiment as the core element and (b) a traditional survey for the parallel and supplementary measurement of additional respondent-specific characteristics, which are used as covariates in the analysis of vignette data. In this chapter, we solely discuss the vignette experiment.

In comparison to traditional survey items, the special design of vignettes enables the simultaneous presentation of several explanatory as well as contextual factors, which leads to more realistic scenarios presented to respondents. As we discuss in detail below, the experimental variation of all vignette factors allows the estimation of unconfounded and context-dependent effects of explanatory vignette factors. For this reason, vignette studies are a very powerful tool for causal investigations of respondent judgements.

The flexibility of vignette studies also supports the realism of vignette measurements. Depending on the research question, vignettes can be presented to respondents in quite different forms, for instance, as text vignettes in keyword, dialogue or narrative style or as cartoons, pictures, audio or video vignettes. Since the mode of stimulus presentation affects individual judgements, the presentation mode must be carefully considered and, if possible, systematically controlled within an experimental setting.

We can further distinguish two types of vignette experiments concerning the amount of stimuli present in the study: we can distinguish between small and large vignette experiments. In large vignette experiments, experiments with vignette populations are too large to be judged by each respondent. Such large vignette populations are typical in some type of survey research and arise when substantive theory does not allow a reduction of the population by dropping some factors or factor levels. Hence, other strategies for restricting the number of vignettes presented to each respondent must be applied. Two strategies are possible: first, the selection of a small sub-sample of the total vignette population, and second, the partitioning of the vignette population into respondent-specific sets. Here the logic is very identical to the design of a fractional design of an experiment.

We are convinced that small vignette experiments are more efficient for most practical applications. The implementation according to an experimental design plan with a deliberate and clear-cut confounding structure allows an accurate and efficient estimation of main and also interaction effects (at least two-way interactions), which are very common for individual judgements and beliefs. For small vignette designs with only a few factors and factor levels (with the same number of factor levels for each factor), experimental vignette designs can be easily constructed – corresponding design plans can be found in the experimental design literature (e.g. Kirk, 1995).

The online version of the vignette experiments is an enriched version of the original because it can deliver information, including vignette content, to research participants through video and audio clips. The use of video and audio clips provides a means of engaging research participants more fully than is possible with written information alone. Videos have previously been used successfully in delivering vignette content (e.g. Arber et al., 2006). The use of video and audio clips to deliver vignette content provides investigators a number of distinct advantages. First, a video format can be helpful in enlisting interest from the subject and assisting the subject in identifying with vignette persons. Video can also be helpful in addressing some of the challenges identified by Wason et al. (2002) in designing vignette content. These challenges include making the vignettes believable, making the manipulated variables obvious and at the same time guarding against framing effects. The use of video to deliver information provides investigators with a way to achieve a good balance between making the manipulated variables clear to research participants and minimizing the risks of framing effects.

Further, the online version of vignette studies provides opportunities for investigators to make interactive options available to research participants before they make judgements. In real-world choice situations, people often have opportunities to seek additional information before they make decisions on complex matters. In the online vignette studies, research participants can be given opportunities to seek information beyond that initially provided by investigators. Opportunities to probe for additional information can be helpful in sustaining the interest of research participants. Further, investigators can record the extent to which respondents took advantage of opportunities to seek additional information. In addition, investigators can record the already discussed metadata and paradata, for example, the amount of time taken by research participants in responding to vignette content. For investigators, it is useful to know how the quantity and kind of information considered influence the judgements made by research participants. Online vignette experiments are experiencing a new life as a form of stated choice studies, thanks to the more interactive forms that the online can offer, increasing considerably their capacity of presenting realistic and complex scenarios that cannot be tested in real-life conditions.

7.3 Framing experiments

Framing experiments are experiments in which research test framing effects. Decisions based on the framing effect are made by focussing on the way the information is presented instead of the information itself. Such decisions may be sub-optimal, as poor information or lesser options can be framed in a positive light. This may make them more attractive than options or information are objectively better, but cast in a less favourable light. Think of someone who unwisely chooses a high-risk investment portfolio because their broker emphasized the upside instead of the potential downside, or a citizen who votes for a protectionist candidate because media coverage has only highlighted the negative repercussions of past trade agreements. The framing effect can have considerable influence on public opinion. Public affairs and other events that draw attention from the public can be interpreted very differently based on how they are framed. Sometimes, issues or positions that benefit most people can be seen unfavourably because of negative framing. Likewise, policy stances and behaviour that do not further the public good may become popular because their positive attributes are effectively emphasized. For example, an overwhelming amount of evidence shows that climate change will result in enormous costs further down the line and that low-income communities will disproportionately bear those costs. Despite this, many citizens deny climate change and believe policies such as carbon taxes will disadvantage the average citizen. This may be because climate change has been framed as a scientifically contentious issue by some media outlets and politicians, who also often highlight the short-term financial costs of environmental policy.

Our choices are influenced by how options are framed through different wordings, reference points and emphasis. The most common framing draws attention to either the positive gain or negative loss associated with an option. We are susceptible to this framing because we tend to avoid loss. The foundational work of psychologists Daniel Kahneman and Amos Tversky explains framing using what they called *prospect theory* (Kahneman and Tversky, 2008).

According to this theory, a loss is perceived as more significant and, therefore, more worthy of avoiding than an equivalent gain. A sure gain is preferred to a probable one, and a probable loss is preferred to a sure loss. Because we want to avoid sure losses, we look for options and information with certain gains. How something is framed can influence our certainty that it will bring either gain or loss. This is why we find it attractive when the positive features of an option are highlighted instead of the negative ones. Processing and evaluating information takes time and energy. To make this process more efficient, our mind often uses shortcuts or 'heuristics'. The availability and affect heuristic may contribute to the framing effect. The availability heuristic is our tendency to use information that comes to mind quickly and easily when making decisions about the future. Studies have shown that the framing effect is more prevalent in older adults with more limited cognitive resources and who therefore favour information that is presented in a way that is easily accessible to them. Because we favour information that is easily understood and recalled, options that are framed in this way are favoured over those that are not.

A simple and typical framing experiment that presents the diagrammatic workflow is presented in Figure 7.3. In this experiment, participants first provide information about themselves and after are randomly assigned to three different groups as prescribed by a between-participants design. The three groups present two possible framing effects selected by the researchers and the control group. In the simplest of implementation, people assigned to the two 'framing groups' are simply first exposed to a message manipulated according to a particular frame, as discussed above.

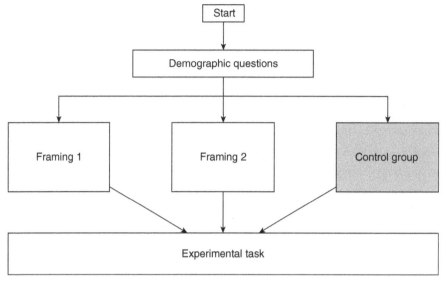

Figure 7.3 Diagrammatic workflow of simple framing experiment

After being exposed to whatever stimuli, all participants will conduct the experimental task. The latter can be anything, including some of the examples that we discuss in this chapter, such as DCEs, Implicit Association Tests (IATs) (or one of its variants) or Behaviour Change Games (BCGs).

Online framing experiments have several features: first, framing can be very interactive, it can be virtually any form of content that people can access and consume online; second, the framing can be easily adapted to support several languages and dynamically assign the right stimuli for each country sample; and third, because of the large population that can be tested, several variations of frames can be tested. Each frame can be designed of subcomponents that can be varied and, therefore, individually tested.

Examples of online framing experiments are common in the scientific literature of online research. Cook et al. (2017) conducted two experiments: one on the effects of inoculation against false media balance and one on its effects against a 'fake experts' technique. Both were designed to expose participants to specific information before completing the subsequent evaluations. In their first experiment, they found that interventions, especially consensus information, had a neutralizing effect on misinformation and especially increased the perceived consensus. Consensus information was also found to have a neutralizing effect on free-market supporters. Concerning the use of 'fake experts', they demonstrated that an inoculation treatment did not protect all respondents against misinformation but especially influenced those who support the free market and 'inoculated' them against misinformation that resonated with their previously held beliefs. However, the effect sizes (in terms of explained variance) that they reported regarding the interaction between inoculation and free-market support were rather small. Interestingly, the inoculation especially protected the perceived consensus, the acceptance of anthropogenic global warming, the attribution of climate change to human influences and the support of mitigation policies for those who support a free market. It had no effect on trust in climate scientists.

Framing experiments online can be easily executed without the need for specific platforms, which might be the case for experiments that require ad hoc programming, like in the case of the IAT or DCE ones. Depending on the experimental task, an online survey platform can be sufficient to implement a framing online experiment if it allows random allocation of participants to the so-called *Split Ballot Testing*. Split Ballot Testing is when you divide your sample (randomly) into two or more sub-samples and perform an experiment. The experiment could be different versions of a survey, different surveys, etc. The goal is to see if any differences exist between the versions of the survey or how users behave differently.

The interesting part of online framing experiments is the possibility of using elements of digital environments as framing. The already mentioned A/B testing that is very common in the industry often refers to the testing of different framing of information on online platforms in order to test the effect that this different framing has on participants. Moreover, researchers can test if the social dimension of many digital environments plays a role by testing the role of information social validation cues on our evaluations, decisions or behaviour. While adding these elements goes beyond the usual scope of framing an experiment, if the object of the experiments is to study online behaviour, researchers can re-create context with great accuracy.

An example of a large-scale online framing experiment is the study conducted by Steinert et al. (2022) on the effectiveness of message framing to increase willingness to vaccinate against COVID-19 in Europe. People were randomly assigned to three different types of messages, framing the advantages of vaccination in different ways. The messages in the experimental conditions were as follows: (i) COVID-19 risk reduction: information about the efficacy of different COVID-19 vaccines, specifically highlighting the effectiveness of vaccines to prevent COVID-19–related deaths and severe disease progressions among vaccinated individuals, relative to unvaccinated individuals; (ii) vaccination certificate: information about exclusive benefits for the vaccinated, including access to travel and leisure activities contingent on providing proof of vaccination in the form of a COVID-19 vaccination certificate; and (iii) hedonistic benefits: information about the prospects of a full restoration of public life and a return to normality, including a wide range of leisure activities (restaurants, theatres, bars, sports, etc.), after population-wide vaccination. In testing these information-based treatments, we found that if you go beyond the average temperature effect (ATE), there is much heterogeneity to the point of detecting 'boomerang effects'. In other words, while we can increase the willingness to vaccinate for many, for some, we decrease it using the same message. The evolution of online framing experiments will largely depend on the creative designs that researchers will develop in the future.

7.4 Implicit attitude test and its variants

In the study of cognitive sociology, the need to capture the implicit aspects of human cognition has popularized a methodology known as the *Implicit Association Test* or *IAT*.

First introduced by Greenwald and colleagues in 1998, the IAT has emerged as one of the most widely used measures of implicit attitudes. Because of its ability to detect biases that are difficult to capture through self-report, it quickly spread beyond psychology and is now widely used in diversity training in both the public and private sectors.

The IAT analyses a subject's automatic evaluations of an object or person based on the idea of 'differential association', which is assessed by measuring the time it takes respondents to associate the visual representation of items (e.g. faces representing race or gender) with evaluations of a certain type (e.g. good or bad). Matching times between items and rating categories predict the existence of an implicit bias or preference towards the rated item: the longer the matching time, the more likely there is a bias towards the item.

The method has come under scrutiny, primarily on three grounds: the validity of the test, the degree to which it predicts discriminatory behaviour and the receptivity of implicit bias to different types of interventions. While the IAT is the subject of considerable controversy among organizational and social psychologists, as well as in the popular press, the consensus is that it outperforms other indirect measures of prejudice in terms of internal validity. In contrast, the debate over the predictive validity of the IAT is not settled: some argue that IAT results correlate with discriminatory behaviour; others argue that the IAT has a limited ability to predict discrimination. Finally, scholars disagree on whether implicit biases are immune to external stimuli.

Regardless of their position in these debates, IAT researchers collectively focus on internal cognitive processes to explain attitudes and judgements, rather than addressing the role of cultural repertoires in structuring prejudice. They implicitly frame cognition as static – regarding 'warm' feelings towards groups, for example – precluding consideration of changes in prejudice over time or context. For example, they do not take into account national variations in the stigmatization of minority groups. Their static understanding of cultural scripts is also reflected in their methods of 'counterbalancing': IAT researchers attempt to limit the impact of what they consider a 'universal norm against darker skin' simply by using grey pixels to represent African Americans.

Although some recognize that the external environment shapes prejudice, IAT researchers typically operationalize context in rather limited ways. For example, the test available on the Project Implicit website (the most important IAT website) incorporates only a few factors, such as the respondent's postal code. The online test asks respondents to provide information on socio-demographic characteristics (e.g. date of birth, race, ethnicity, gender and political identity), but does not collect data on contextual factors that are likely to influence the nature of prejudice, such as the frequency of interaction with the groups presented in the test (e.g. the number of minorities living in one's neighbourhood) or the extent to which an ethno-racial group is stigmatized in the subject's environment. Not taking into account important information about available cultural repertoires limits the ability of IAT researchers to understand the social significance of implicit biases.

Neglecting the cultural repertoires that underlie cognitive processes has important consequences. One of these is that IAT research cannot specify the meaning of differential associations. Above all, researchers cannot determine whether the speed of association between categories of images and words is due to positive and negative evaluation or to relative exposure and familiarity. Information about prior exposure to cultural repertoires is needed to determine whether a shorter association time is due to lack of exposure to the designated item or an actual reflection of a bias against it.

Documenting predominant schemas can help IAT scholars distinguish salience-driven outcomes from evaluation-driven outcomes. Interdisciplinary collaboration could further enhance research by building on the work of scholars who examine how socially constructed logics drive internal cognitive processes. While sociologists can better understand how culture works by considering automatic cognition in their analyses, we propose that collaboration would also benefit IAT researchers by providing opportunities to refine their findings and interpretations of their results. The IAT has been, in any case, what one might call a development platform for other methodologies that are derivations of it. In the next section, we discuss one of these, namely, the concept association task (CAT).

7.4.1 The concept association task

A particularly promising measure of implicit cognitive and cultural schemas is the concept association task (CAT) recently developed by Hunzaker (2017). In this task, respondents are shown concepts related to a given topic two at a time and asked to indicate whether they are related. Before starting the task, respondents are told that the concepts might be related because 'one causes the other' or because 'they commonly go together for some other reason', prompting them to think about relatedness in broad terms (p. 355). To increase confidence in automatic processing, respondents are instructed to respond quickly and using their initial instincts. All possible pairwise combinations of concepts are assessed in this way, excluding logically inconsistent pairs. CAT is time-consuming (e.g. averaging 33 minutes to assess 490 concept pairs), but the result is data on the entire network of conceptual associations that can be analyzed using any of the myriad of network methods designed to identify central or structurally equivalent concepts, isolate groups (i.e. subcultural understandings) and so on. These data are direct measures of associations at the individual level, which means that they can be used not only to detect cultural patterns, as relational class analysis (RCA) and correlation class analysis (CCA) do, but also to probe individual variation in schematic representations. Further- more, CAT can be adapted to capture associations between any set of concepts, but this places the burden on the researcher to accu- rately identify the concepts that apply to a given topic. Although this determination could be done a posteriori, suggesting a 'let's include it and see if it is important' approach, this will generally be imprac- tical in practice because each new concept must be matched with all other concepts, which substantially increases the response burden on participants.

CAT instructs participants to rely on instinct and to respond quickly, which should make it easier to catch automatic processes.

The motivation to consciously check responses is likely to be low, as respondents are instructed to state whether concepts are related (but not why), and because it is not obvious from the task instructions how the data will be used. These features alone, however, do not guarantee automatic processing because they do not necessarily capture unintentional or uncontrolled responses. To solve this problem, the task data could be supplemented with response times for each concept pair. These could be used to identify and remove individuals who are likely to have reflected on their responses (as suggested by the high response times) or incorporated directly into the analyses. In a network analysis, for example, response times could be used as weights on the links between concepts. Using the same logic as in IAT data, response times should be largely uncontrollable and reflect the strength of cognitive associations. Therefore, the use of response times in analyses would increase the likelihood that the results reflect the functioning of automatic processes. Response time data could be made even more useful by modifying the task to allow respondents to answer using the keyboard rather than mouse clicks. This would increase the speed of responses and make it more difficult for deliberative processes to intervene.

One example of the use of IAT is a recent work by Reuben and colleagues (Reuben et al., 2014). In their study about stereotypes that impedes women career in science, they uncovered implicit stereotypes in their respondents using the IAT test. All subjects are to complete an IAT associating sex with science-related abilities. In the context of this study, the authors used an IAT that required subjects to associate words/pictures with the categories 'male', 'female', 'math and science' and 'liberal arts'. In one condition, subjects used the same key to categorize items representing male (e.g. a picture of a man) and math/science (e.g. the word 'calculus') and another key to categorize items representing female (e.g. a picture of a woman) and liberal arts (e.g. the word 'literature'). In the other condition, subjects categorized the same words/pictures, but the words and pictures were paired differently: Male and liberal arts appeared together, and female and math/science items appeared together. Most people categorize the words/pictures faster and more accurately in the male–math/science condition than the female–math/science condition. This difference is interpreted as reflecting an implicit sex–math/science stereotype such that males are seen as more capable in these fields. The results indicated that employers with a stronger implicit bias against women were more willing to believe men's over-estimated expectations of their future performance.

7.5 Games

Gamification is a term coined in 2008 in the digital media industry. Before the second half of 2010, parallel terms with the same concept have been widely adopted such as 'behavioural games', 'playful design', 'surveillance entertainment', 'productivity games' and 'funware'. Gamification is defined as follows: 'Effective gamification is influencing human behaviour through engaging experiences, using game design principles in decision-making applications and services'. Others have defined gamification as the adoption of the methods of game design and game technology outside of the games industry. It is often associated with behavioural research, where game elements can be used to promote certain behaviour. Its application has spread rapidly in technology and health domains. Though both terms, gamification and serious games, have been frequently used together in many studies, they are different approaches in terms of the way they work. Gamification blends the game mechanics with traditional activities, for example, learning and physical activity. However, serious games not only follow the typical game structure but also aim to achieve the goal that the game is built for, such as changing attitudes or behaviours.

Serious games aimed at changing attitudes or behaviours are called *Behaviour Change Games* or *BCG*. BCGs form a subset of serious games, which were designed to support attitude and change behaviours. BCG have the same nature as what are often called *persuasive games*. Persuasive technology is defined as 'an interactive product designed to change attitudes or behaviours by making desired outcomes easier to achieve'. Naturally, video games are used to implement persuasive strategies by utilizing the power of mechanics and elements of the game design; for instance, self-monitoring, which can allow people to monitor themselves; conditioning, which offers rewards based on the performance of particular behaviour; and tunnelling, which is about leading players through a prearranged sequence of actions to either encourage or discourage particular behaviour. Persuasive games have applications in many fields, such as health games, political and social games and advertising games aiming to change behaviour regarding certain issues, such as encouraging recycling, discouraging smoking or increasing voting.

Game features can be categorized into mechanics and components. According to Bharathi et al. (2016), game design features are relevant to mechanics, for example, challenges, feedback and rewards, and components, for example, achievements, avatars, badges, leaderboards, levels, points and social graphs, as well as latent game design features. To be more focussed on BCGs or persuasive games, game design elements and mechanics vary based on the type of gamified application and the desired outcome, that is, whether they are built for learning purposes, health behaviours or fitness purposes. Examples of features of BCGs are as follows:

- Daily log-in bonus: Players get a bonus every day they log in.
- Levels: Serious games are often based on levels. When players get better, they reach a higher level, which keeps the game challenging.
- Rewards: Successful actions are rewarded with in-game rewards (such as points).
- Leaderboards: A visual representation (ranking) that allows players to compete with each other.
- Feedback: Players receive direct feedback. Even if a wrong decision has been made, a game ensures that the player will understand this without feeling attacked.

For instance, in health applications, the game design incorporates several strategies, such as monitoring, harmony, group opinion and dis-establishing. In fitness applications, game design has been used to encourage players' long-term engagement through social inter-action. Therefore, different elements and mechanics such as social play, micro goals, fair play and marginal challenge are often employed.

An example of a successful BCG is Powerhouse, a game developed at Stanford University and designed as an intervention to change people's behaviour regarding energy consumption (Reeves et al., 2015). Powerhouse targets the average American homeowner. Powerhouse utilizes a high degree of interactivity in order to encourage a high degree of player investment, community involve-ment and behaviour change. The interactivity takes the form of a player controlling the actions of a virtual resident within a virtual home. The player travels from room to room discovering ways for the virtual resident to save energy within the house. For example, the player guides the resident to an unoccupied yet fully lit room. After switching the lights off, points are awarded to the player (earning him/her an Achievements Badge) and the player's energy dashboard is updated accordingly. The virtual home's energy usage trends are then compared to the player's real-time energy use within their actual home. Therefore, Stanford researchers can understand whether there is a direct link between a player's efforts to decrease energy in the virtual home with their actual energy consumption behaviours. These competing graphs are even overlaid, which enables the player to see his or her virtual usage as compared to his or her actual. Another main component of Powerhouse is the Forum feature. This feature encourages an individual player to connect with other players. Players can ask questions amongst each other, post interesting things they learned and engage the Stanford research group themselves. Not only are these actions encouraged but they are even required for level advancement. In order to pass from one section to another, for example, a player must post within the forum, 'friend' the Stanford administrator's avatar and speculate on why their energy use either increased or decreased during a particular section. There are BCGs that resemble Powerhouse, for example, 'SimpleEnergy' developed in the commercial sector.

In general, there are many examples of BCGs in the current scientific literature and their development shows great promises that serious gaming for behaviour change holds for the society – be it for inclusion and empowerment of minorities such as autistic children or migrants or for training on the job or cases of emergency. It further made it evident that behaviour and affect analysis of the users' can lead to provision of corrective feedback alongside adapting the progress of the game's difficulty in a motivational way. Fully automatic affective and behavioural analysis and fully automatic in-game feedback are possible with today's technology. In particular, pervasive solutions can train the user in a playful way in everyday life standard situations and allow close-to-real-life simulations.

7.6 Chapter summary

In this chapter, we have presented different forms of online experiments and discussed the following topics:

- We introduced several implementations of online experiments: choice experiments, vignette studies, framing experiments, IAT-based experiments and serious gaming studies.
- First, we have discussed the underlying rationale of choice experiments and their implementation online. DCE is an attribute-based survey method for measuring benefits (utility). DCEs present respondents with samples of hypothetical scenarios (choice sets) extracted a priori from all possible choice sets according to statistical design principles.
- Next, we presented and discussed the main features of vignette studies and how they can be conducted online. Researchers in the CVT approach to examine how vignette structure influences responses. In its simplest form, it randomly presents minimally contrastive versions of a single vignette (story) to respondents. The minimal contrasts allow experimenters to investigate how the manipulation of a single factor influences respondents' judgements.

- Framing experiments are also a popular form of online experiments. Our choices are influenced by how options are framed through different wordings, reference points and emphasis. A simple and typical framing experiment has participants first provide information about themselves and then be randomly assigned to three different groups as prescribed by a between-participants design. Framing experiments online can be easily executed without the need for specific platforms, which might be the case for experiments that require ad hoc programming, like in the case of the IAT or DCE ones.

- Implicit cognition of individuals is increasingly important in social science, and IAT-based experiments are also very popular. They are meant to identify implicit biases that people might have and are often combined with other experiments like the DCE discussed previously.

- Serious games aimed at changing attitudes or behaviours are called *Behaviour Change Games* or *BCG*. BCGs form a subset of serious games, which were designed in order to support attitude and change behaviours. Game features can be categorized into mechanics and components. Game design features are relevant to mechanics, for example, challenges, feedback and rewards, and components, for example, achievements, avatars, badges, leaderboards, levels, points and social graphs, as well as latent game design features.

Further readings

In this chapter, we discussed several experiments, each with its scientific literature. Hence, we limit our suggestions to what we consider valid introductory texts. For choice experiments:

- Zwerina's *Discrete Choice Experiments in Marketing* (2000) is a good text for all sorts of social scientists;

- Aizaki et al.'s *Stated Preferences Methods Using R* (2015) is an excellent but more technical resource. It is probably the most recent and complete book on choice experiments and their analysis;

- also relevant is Chorus's *Random Regret-based Discrete Choice Modeling* (2012), which is one of the few books about the random regret approach to DCEs.

Moving to vignette studies, while the topic is present in many books we have already suggested in previous sections, the best current book remains Auspurg and Hinz's *Factorial Survey Experiments* (2014). As far as we know, there are no specific books on framing experiments. However, in many psychology-oriented books about experimental methods, framing experiments are often the preferred choice as an example. A similar situation is actual for IAT-based experiments. Again, no specific book exists, but several excellent books about measuring implicit cognition or preferences discuss the use of IAT and its derivates (like the conceptual association task discussed in this book). We have the book edited by Wittenbrink and Schwartz, *Implicit Measures of Attitudes* (2007), and the *Handbook of Implicit Social Cognition: Measurement, Theory, and Applications* edited by Gawronski and Payne (2010).

Serious games and game-based experiments are a new method; in this case, there is no specific book about designing them. However, few books about gamification also discuss potential experimental designs. We have the volume *Gamification: Using Game Elements in Serious Contexts,* edited by Stieglitz et al. (2018). More focussed on design aspects and more directed to practitioners, there is Chou's *Actionable Gamification: Beyond Points, Badges, and Leaderboards* (2015). A more general reflection on the topic is the excellent book by Jagoda, *Experimental Games: Critique, Play, and Design in the Age of Gamification* (2021).

8

THE VALUE OF POPULATION-BASED SURVEY EXPERIMENTS FOR SOCIAL SCIENTIFIC RESEARCH

―――――― Chapter objectives ――――――

- To outline the role of online experiments, in the form of randomized controlled trial, in the social science
- To understand the specific potential provided by the large-scale online experiment findings for the social science
- To reconsider the debate about external validity in light of the innovation introduced by online experiments

―――――― Key concepts ――――――

- Experiments in randomized controlled trial (RCT) forms prevent social scientists from engaging in post-factum interpretations. Online RCTs

(Continued)

are much more implementable compared to the past, thanks to online.

- Harnessing heterogeneity in large online experiments is a viable research strategy using computational social science methods such as model-based recursive partitioning.
- Experiments vary in their degree of 'fieldness' along several dimensions, from the setting in which the experiment takes place (lab versus real world) to the authenticity of the treatment, participants, context and outcome measures.

8.1 Encouraging experiments in the social sciences

Experiments have been, for a long time, common only in a subset of the social sciences, but in the past at least 20 years, their adoption has reached many of the disciplines within the social science domain. It is not unusual to encounter experiments in political science research or sociology, while experimental economics is now an established field. It is likely that there are multiple reasons for this renewed interest. The logic of experimentation – which entails assessing the effect of an intervention by comparing the outcomes of two or more conditions – is very intuitive. Less obvious, until the development of modern statistics, has been the importance of random assignment for assessing causal effects. Indeed, random assignment is the most important feature of experimental design. When participants are effectively randomized to treatment conditions, their characteristics are similarly distributed across these conditions, making it possible to exclude the possibility of unobserved confounders and thereby assess the true causal effect of an intervention. In fact, one of the main attractive aspects of an experiment is that is a research method that does need all potential confounders to be considered to make causal statements. The second reason of the renewed interest is the increased emphasis on establishing causal relations and assessments in the context of doing social science research. This emphasis comes from different sources but, we believe, a major role is a pressure of applying research to test solutions to societal issues. Rigorous causal assessment is vital for social interventions. If we want to lift people out of poverty or increase voting turnout, we need to know which interventions will produce change.

This is likely the reason for the increased popularity of randomized controlled trial (RCT) that is one of the most common forms of experiments in the social sciences. Long regarded as the gold standard in clinical research, RCTs have made their way into many applied fields in the social sciences. In an RCT, researchers randomly assign participants to one or more treatment conditions and evaluate the effectiveness of the intervention by comparing treated participants with those in a control group (or those who received a different treatment).

The problem was that the methods used to be able to isolate the impact of a cause on an effect were implemented using somewhat arbitrary hypotheses, with the result that small variations in the hypotheses sometimes led to completely different inferences.

The fascination for experiments with random assignment to the treatment and control group (RCT) also arose as a response to this dissatisfaction. The importance of the experiment is revealed in the increasing use with which it is used in the social sciences, with the aim of calculating an impact ceteris paribus. A simple way of thinking about the problem of causal identification is to use the concept of the potential outcome. Suppose we want to see whether a public policy of distributing washing machines to women promotes female participation in the labour market. It is possible to think of the potential outcome as the probability for the woman to offer work outside the home, in the absence and presence of the washing machine. We could also collect data on households with and without a washing machine, but we would not be sure that the set of women with and without a washing machine is on average equal: could it not be that it is women who are already working, or with higher educational qualifications and therefore more likely to work, who buy the washing machine? Distributing washing machines by means of a lottery ensures that any characteristics (age, laziness, number of children, educational qualification, etc.) that may influence the labour supply do not differ on average between those who win the washing machine and those who do not. In this way, those who do not receive the washing machine allow us (on average) to see what would have happened to those who did if they had not. Selection bias is defined as the possibility that the potential outcome of those who already have the washing machine is different from those who do not. The RCT distributing washing machines through a lottery is one way of solving the selection problem.

Some RCTs applied to public policies are milestones of recent empirical analysis. Social policies were 'revolutionized' by the case of Progresa in Mexico (Parker and Todd, 2017). In that case, the random allocation of the conditional grant or rather the deferral of payment to some randomly chosen households led to a rigorous assessment of benefits. Another symbolic programme is STAR (discussed in Chapter 1): a public policy in Tennessee (USA) where primary schools children were randomly assigned to different class sizes (Finn and Achilles, 1990).

Recent RCTs have dramatically shifted the debate on poverty reduction from theorizing about the importance of foreign aid or the quality of political institutions towards a straightforward question: What works and what does not work in fighting poverty? Carefully designed RCTs favour the reliable identification of intervention effects in the face of complex and multiple channels of causality. As a result, RCTs have become the gold standard for policy evaluation in important circles.

Scholars have articulated several interrelated criticisms of the RCT method. First, what makes RCTs popular – their attention to what works – is, according to some social scientists, a manifestation of the trend towards the so-called atheoretical work. RCTs, they contend, focus on whether, rather than why, programmes work (Deaton, 2010). However, a counterargument is offered by Banerjee and Duflo (2011) in their book on the economics of poverty, make a strenuous defence of RCTs applied to projects and policies in developing countries, comparing them to the revolution these tools have brought to medicine. The methodological break is also a theoretical break. Enough of the big debates on the role of institutions or development aid, the two economists argue, better to focus on projects and small issues and see, with experimental evidence, whether they work.

In general, however, the criticism towards RCTs does not take issue with the experimental method itself, but with what is being investigated, namely, intervention programmes instead of theoretically derived hypotheses and mechanisms. Being able to answer whether an intervention works but not why it works seriously limits the generalizability of the findings and hence the capacity to successfully export that intervention to other contexts.

Another aspect of experiments that has been object of criticism because they limit researchers' ability to draw inferences and extrapolate from RCT results is treatment heterogeneity, that is, the fact that treatment effects may vary across participants. To be clear, even in the presence of treatment heterogeneity, randomization allows for the reliable estimation of the average treatment effect (ATE) (Cox, 1958; Gerber and Green, 2012). In fact, what makes experiments particularly valuable is that we do not need to assume that the treatment effect is the same on all participants to have an unbiased estimate of the ATE.

However, as soon as we turn our attention to questions related to the distribution of that effect – for example, the proportion of people who benefit from an intervention, whether certain subgroups (e.g. male) are more responsive to the intervention or whether the intervention adversely affects some people – we expose ourselves to the possibility of biased estimates. The ability of extrapolating findings and information on treatment heterogeneity and subgroup analyses are vital for intervention implementation, programme scale-up and generalization to larger or different populations. When the effect is not constant across individuals but varies systematically with covariates, we need to make additional assumptions in order to generalize RCT results beyond the setting and participants of the experiment. Such assumptions can rely on theory, previous knowledge or additional experimentation. According to Deaton (2010), the risk is that RCTs that are not theoretically guided can be difficult to extend to more than local validity. The issue of heterogeneity of treatment will be under our attention in the next section where we will discuss new developments that can help with this aspect of experiments.

Experiments remain important to the improvement of social sciences. Above all, the use of experiments limits the use of post-factum interpretations by social scientists. The only hypotheses researchers can test in the context of field experiments are those formulated by the researcher ex ante, during the research design phase. Sociologists are skilled at coming up with plausible explanations for observed correlations. The problem with interpretations after the fact is that they are often ad hoc and do not prompt the researcher to further investigations. By contrast, field experimental methods serve to channel research towards a virtuous circle of inquiry, in which theories are explicitly specified, evaluated and refined incrementally. Concerns about generalizability, along with those about treatment heterogeneity and scalability, are not specific to field experiments. In fact, they probably come up more often in the context of experimental, rather than observational, research because other inferential problems have been effectively addressed. They affect all empirical research, albeit in different ways. However, when field experimenters proceed through replication and repetition – tasks to which the method is suited – they are in a strong position to address these issues.

The last point of encouraging the use of experiments is because the method is now ubiquitous across the social sciences, experiments enable social scientists to participate in interdisciplinary research programmes. The social scientist who masters field experiments is positioned to engage psychologists, economists and political scientists on questions of enduring social scientific interest and policy relevance, from the effects of online dark patterns and the building blocks of cooperation to the most effective strategies to support people's decisions about their pensions.

8.2 Heterogeneous treatment effects and population-based survey experiment

In Chapter 1, we have illustrated the debate around the issue of external validity as one of the shortcomings of laboratory experiments that can be solved using online ones. We also have discussed in Chapter 4 the possible sampling strategies in the context of combining the strengths of online survey sampling techniques with the elicitation of an online experiment. In particular, using a large sample drawn from traditional sampling frames, such as tax records, and employed in online experimental studies has consequences on what is possible to pursue in terms of analytical strategy.

Extending experiments to large samples, both national and international, increases the potential heterogeneity present in response to our treatments. Therefore, identifying and studying such heterogeneity is a crucial step in the world of online behavioural experiments. New analytical techniques have emerged in computational and computer sciences that are very promising to achieve this goal. One of the best examples of how social science can benefit from analytical approaches developed in computational methods is the development of model-based recursive partitioning (MBRP). This approach improves the use of classification and regression trees (CART). The latter also is a method from the 'algorithmic culture' of modelling that has valuable applications in the social sciences but is essentially data driven (Berk, 2006; Hand and Vinciotti, 2003).

In summary, CART are based on a purely data-driven paradigm. Without using a predefined statistical model, such algorithmic methods recursively search for groups of observations with similar response variable values by constructing a tree structure. Thus, they are instrumental in data exploration and express their best utility in the context of very complex and large datasets. However, such techniques make no use of theory in describing a pattern of how the data were generated and are purely descriptive, although far superior to the 'traditional' descriptive statistics used in the social sciences when dealing with large datasets.

MBRP (Zeileis et al., 2008) represents a synthesis of a theoretical approach and a set of data-driven constraints for theory validation and further development. In summary, this approach works through the following steps. Firstly, a parametric model is defined to express a set of theoretical assumptions (e.g. through a linear regression). Second, this model is evaluated according to the recursive partitioning algorithm, which checks whether other important covariates that would alter the parameters of the initial model have been omitted. Third, the same regression or classification tree structure is produced. This time, instead of partitioning by different patterns of the response variable, MBRP finds different patterns of associations between the response variable and other covariates that have been pre-specified in the parametric model. In other words, it creates different versions of the parametric model in terms of beta (β) estimation, depending on the different important values of the covariates. (For the technical aspects of how this is done, see Zeileis and Hornik, 2007.) In other words, the presence of splits indicates that the parameters of the initial theory-driven definition are unstable, and that the data are too heterogeneous to be explained by a single global model. The model does not describe the entire dataset.

The use of this computational method follows these steps:

1 Once you have the data, define a model to predict the outcome variable object of your study. This model can be linear or logistic, it does not matter.
2 If you have a model, the next step is to run the algorithm to check if your model behaves in the same way across subsets of your sample defined by some covariates (often, these are socio-demographic variables, but it can be other types of segmenting variables).
3 The MBRP technique will produce a tree presentation with splits if there is a statistically significant difference in how a model is for one group of people with a given value of a covariate compared to the rest.

Figure 8.1 presents an example of that what is discussed above. The tree representation shows the variation of an experimental manipulation effect according to two covariates. This online experiment was about testing the effect of showing a particular message in increasing people's willingness to get vaccinated against COVID-19. In this simplified example, we had two covariates, the level of exposure to misinformation (misinfo_f_hedo) and if people were subject to a curfew (curfew_f_hedo). The bottom box represents the

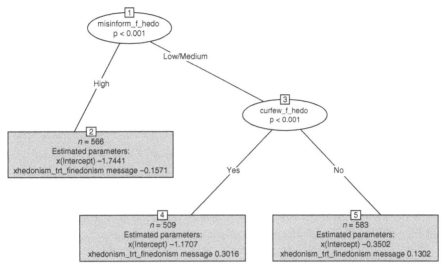

Figure 8.1 Example of a partitioning approach applied to an online experiment

terminal nodes, in other words, the subgroups identified by the MBRP are 3, namely nodes 2, 4 and 5. The variable measuring our experimental treatment (our message) is xhedonism_trt and what we can see is that it has different estimates in the three nodes: in node 2, it is negative, meaning that for this group of people it had a negative effect; for nodes 4 and 5, it is positive although the effect is much stronger for node 4 than 5. Nodes here are nothing else that subgroups of our participants characterized by a given combination of the values of the covariates. For example, node 4 represents people who had low exposure to disinformation and had a curfew experience.

MBRP was developed as an advancement of CART. Both methods originate from machine learning, which is influenced by both statistics and computer science, and they are the so-called CART methods.

Classification trees look for different patterns in the response variable based on the available covariates. Since the sample is divided into rectangular partitions defined by the values of the covariates and since the same covariate can be selected for several partitions, classification trees can also evaluate complex interactions, non-linear and non-monotonic patterns. Furthermore, the structure of the underlying data generation process is not specified in advance but is determined in an entirely data-driven way. These are the key distinctions between classification and regression trees and classical regression models.

Classification and regression trees are purely data-driven and exploratory – and thus mark the complete opposite of the model specification theory approach prevalent in the empirical social sciences. However, the advanced MBRP method combines the advantages of both approaches: at first, a parametric model is formulated to represent a theory-driven research hypothesis. Then this parametric model is handed over to the MBRP algorithm, which checks whether other relevant covariates have been omitted that would alter the model parameters of interest.

Technically, the tree structure obtained from the classification and regression trees remains the same for MBRP. However, the application of MBRP offers new impulses for research in the social, educational and behavioural sciences. For the interpretation of MBRP, we would like to emphasize the connection to the principle of parsimony: following the fundamental research paradigm that theories developed in the social sciences must produce falsifiable hypotheses, these are translated into statistical models. The aim of model building is thus to simplify complex reality. What is the advantage of having such information? The answer to this question relates to the initial distinction that was introduced about the two modelling cultures. In the predominant (in the social sciences) data modelling culture, comparing different models has always been complex and problematic. The hybrid approach of MBRP modelling can help review models that work for the whole dataset and do not neglect such information that imposes on the models as 'global' straitjackets.

In applying MBRP in the context of experiments, assuming an RTC, researchers have adjusted the method for this purpose, introducing the notion of an 'honest tree'. The notion of *honest* stems from building the tree structure on a training sample and the estimate of the leafs on an estimation sample. Here, we use sub-sample A as the training data and sub-sample B as the estimation sample. Note that we do not need to explicitly formulate the interactions. This is exactly the benefit of tree-based methods. In this context, the next evolution (Figure 8.2) are the two following approaches:

Causal Tree (Athey and Imbens, 2016): A data-driven approach to partition the data into subpopulations that differ in the magnitude of their treatment effects. The approach enables the construction of valid confidence intervals for treatment effects.

Causal Forests (Wager and Athey, 2018) and the R-learner (Nie and Wager, 2017): Causal forests is a specialization of the *generalized random forests* algorithm to estimate conditional average treatment effects, with its implementation motivated by the R-learner. The R-learner is a meta-algorithm used to combine different supervised learning algorithms to produce better estimates of conditional average treatment effects.

Moreover, there is also a Bayesian approach, the Bayesian Additive Regression Trees or BART (Green and Kern, 2012). BART is a sum-of-trees model for approximating an unknown function f. BART uses a regularization prior that forces each tree to be able to explain only a limited subset of the relationships between the covariates and the predictor variable.

Another valuable piece of information generated by this approach is that the recursive model-based method allows for identifying particular segments of the sample under investigation that might merit further investigation. That is, the possibility of identifying segments of our sample (and, therefore, presumably segments of the population if our sample is representative) that have a different version of the general theoretical model we have employed, in the form of statistical regression, to explain a given phenomenon Y. This possibility of identifying 'local' models of the population is not just a matter of chance. When applied to independent variables involving the measurement of attitudes and preferences, this possibility of

Figure 8.2 Evolution of recursive portioning methods in the context of experimental and observational data

identifying 'local' models as defined above allows us to identify subgroups characterized by a particular cognitive pattern shared by that group. Such a group could very well be transversal to traditional socio-demographic categories (the young, the old, the middle class, etc.). Applied to experiments, it represents an advanced form of heterogeneity of treatment effects analysis that, with sufficient cases, can be very informative about the presence of general and local effects of treatments.

This approach is very promising but has a 'cost' in methodological terms. It needs large samples and, even better, samples collected in several countries to work well. Only with a sufficient number of cases, we can identify noteworthy subgroups. In contrast, if we have a few hundred cases, we cannot be sure of the statistical validity of the partitioning, besides the fact that we are talking about subgroups consisting of a few tens of cases that are uninteresting as results.

From the perspective of how this exploitation of heterogeneity can be harnessed, it will largely depend on the type of experiments and phenomena we study. For example, in the case of the author of this book, the online experiments conducted were about testing the effect of treatments in terms of behavioural change and identifying the heterogeneity of the treatment effects allowed researchers to define specific strategies for a particular subset of the population to avoid boomerang effects (to obtain the opposite effect of what was intended).

8.3 External validity reconsidered

One of the most attractive selling points of online experiments compared to lab ones is the already discussed issue of external validity. At this point, it should be clear that an online experiment is just a term that hides a plethora of diverse implementations. The large amount of variations that online environments offer is continuously updated by the emergence of new platforms and technologies and that, in turn, affects the possibilities of new forms of online experiments. Their degree of external validity but of internal and ecological ones can vary according to the implementation that an online experiment can take. In this respect, it is useful to frame the issue like Gerber and Green's (2012) position, according to which experiments vary in their degree of 'fieldness' along several dimensions, from the setting in which the experiment takes place (lab versus real world) to the authenticity of the treatment, participants, context and outcome measures.

Such degree of fieldness does vary a lot for online experiments, given the pervasiveness of the digital in our lives. We are increasingly always online; therefore, the idea of distributing or eliciting an online experiment simply having participants sitting in front of a PC represents the full picture. The use of smartphones, tablets and now wearable devices, all interconnected among them, creates the unprecedented opportunity of eliciting stimuli by combining different devices in different contexts. Such possibilities include additional dimensions, such as the obtrusiveness of the data collection process.

We have previously discussed the role of further data forms such as paradata and metadata. With the use of a device like a smartphone that includes sensors and can be carried everywhere, online and field experiments can merge into a hybrid form that is still entirely to develop.

Moreover, one way of increasing the validity of experimental results is by combining distinct experimental as well as observational methods, aka 'cross-validation' or 'empirical cross-checking' (see Barr et al., 2021). It means employing different research designs allows for complementary tests of the same hypotheses or for complementary ways of establishing empirical regularities. Doing so contributes to the robustness of empirical findings and ultimately to cumulative knowledge. Indeed, experimental cross-validation is becoming more frequent. Some studies have combined laboratory with online experimental designs (Sarsons et al., 2021); others have combined laboratory with vignette and observational data (Chen and Tam, 2020) or variations, such as laboratory with vignette (Barr et al., 2021), vignette with observational data (Eifler, 2010; Petzold and Wolbring, 2019) or laboratory with audit designs (Correll et al., 2007).

Online experiments are no longer mainly an academic tool. The tech industry, particularly the so-called big tech, widely employs online experiments, they are called 'A/B testing' (Control A and Treatment B). However, they are exactly the same of controlled online experiments as discussed in this book. Online controlled experiments are used heavily in companies like Airbnb, Amazon, Booking.com, eBay, Facebook, Google, LinkedIn, Lyft, Microsoft, Netflix, Twitter, Uber, Yahoo!/Oath and Yandex (Gupta et al., 2019). These companies run thousands to tens of thousands of experiments every year, sometimes involving millions of users and testing everything, including changes to the user interface, relevance algorithms (search, ads, personalization, recommendations and so on), latency/performance, content management systems, customer support systems and more. Experiments are run on multiple channels: websites, desktop applications, mobile applications and email. They focus on the OEC, the overall evaluation criterion, a quantitative measure of the experiment's objective.

The future of online experiments is very fluid, the degree of fieldness that will be possible to obtain is still undetermined but the potential appears to be intriguing. The merging of the characteristics of online and field experiments into one and new hybrid forms is likely to be the next evolution of this form of data collection.

REFERENCES

Acquisti, A., Brandimarte, L., & Loewenstein, G. (2015). Privacy and human behavior in the age of information. *Science, 347*(6221), 509e514.

Aizaki, H., Nakatani, T., & Sato, K. (2015). *Stated preference methods using r*. London: Taylor & Francis.

Arber, S., McKinlay, J., Adams, A., Marceau, L., Link, C., & O'Donnell, A. (2006). Patient characteristics and inequalities in doctors' diagnostic and management strategies relating to CHD: A video-simulation experiment. *Social Science & Medicine, 62*, 103–115.

Aronson, E., Phoebe, C., Ellsworth, J., Carlsmith, M., & Gonzales, M. (1990). *Methods of research in social psychology* (2nd ed.). New York, NY: McGraw-Hill.

Athey, S., & Imbens, G. (2016). Recursive partitioning for heterogeneous causal effects. *Proceedings of the National Academy of Sciences, 113*(27), 7353–7360. https://doi.org/10.1073/pnas.1510489113

Barr, A., Miller, L., & Ubeda, P. (2021). Is the acknowledgment of earned entitlement effect robust across experimental modes and populations? *Sociological Methods & Research*. https://doi.org/10.1177/0049124120986194

Batinic, B., Reips, U., & Bosnjak, M. (Eds.). (2000). *Online social sciences*. Seattle, WA: Hogrefe and Huber.

Batinic, B., Reips, U.-D., & Bosnjak, M. (Eds.). (2002). *Online social sciences*. Hogrefe & Huber Publishers.

Bharathi, A. K. B. G., Singh, A., Tucker, C. S., & Nembhard, H. B. (2016). Knowledge discovery of game design features by mining user-generated feedback. *Computers in Human Behavior, 60*, 361–371.

Birnbaum, M. H. (2004). Human research and data collection via the internet. *Annual Review of Psychology, 55*, 803–832.

Birnbaum, M. H. (2004b). Human research and data collection via the internet. *Annual Review of Psychology, 55*, 803–832.

Brand, J. E., Xu, J., Koch, B., & Geraldo, P. (2021). Uncovering sociological effect heterogeneity using tree-based machine learning. *Sociological Methodology, 51*(2), 189–223. https://doi.org/10.1177/0081175021993503

Bronfenbrenner, U. (1977). Toward an experimental ecology of human development. *American Psychologist, 32*, 513–531.

Brunswik, E. (1943). Organismic achievement and environmental probability. *Psychological Review, 50*, 255–272.

Burns, M. N., Begale, M., Duffecy, J., Gergle, D., Karr, C. J., Giangrande, E., & Mohr, D. C. (2011). Harnessing context sensing to develop a mobile intervention for depression. *Journal of Medical Internet Research, 13*, e55.

Busemeyer, J. R., & Townsend, J. T. (1992). Fundamental derivations from decision field theory. *Mathematical Social Sciences, 23*(3), 255–282.

Busemeyer, J. R., & Townsend, J. T. (1993). Decision field theory: A dynamic-cognitive approach to decision making in an uncertain environment. *Psychological Review, 100*(3), 432.

Campbell, D. T. (1957). Factors relevant to the validity of experiments in social settings. *Psychological Bulletin, 54*(4), 297–312.

Campbell, D. T., & Stanley, J. (1966). *Experimental and quasi-experimental evaluations in social research.* Chicago, IL: Rand McNally.

Centola, D. (2010). The spread of behavior in an online social network experiment. *Science, 329*(5996), 1194–1197.

Chen, J. C., & Tam, T. (2020). Uses of artificial and composite treatments in experimental methods: Reconsidering the problem of validity and its implications for stratification research. *Research in Social Stratification and Mobility, 65.*

Chorus, C. G. (2012). *Random regret-based discrete choice modelling: A tutorial.* Berlin: Springer.

Chou, Yu-K. (2019). *Actionable gamification.* PACKT Publishing Limited.

Christian, L. M., Dillman, D. A., & Smyth, J. D. (2007). Helping respondents get it right the first time: The influence of words, symbols, and graphics in web surveys. *Public Opinion Quarterly, 71*(1), 113–125.

Comley, P. (2000). Pop-up surveys: What works, what doesn't work and what will work in the future. *Proceedings of the ESOMAR Worldwide Internet Conference Net Effects 3 (Vol. 237).* Amsterdam, NL: ESOMAR. www.virtualsurveys.com/news/papers/paper_4.asp. Accessed on October 15, 2022.

Cook, T., & Campbell, D. (1979). *Quasi-experimentation: Design and analysis for field settings.* Chicago, IL: Rand McNally.

Cook, J., Lewandowsky, S., & Ecker, U. K. H. (2017). Neutralizing misinformation through inoculation: Exposing misleading argumentation techniques reduces their influence. *PLOS ONE, 12*(5), e0175799. https://doi.org/10.1371/journal.pone.0175799

Correll, J. S., Benard, S., & Paik, I. (2007). Getting a job: Is there a motherhood penalty? *American Journal of Sociology, 112*, 1297–1339.

Couper, M. (1998). Measuring survey quality in a CASIC environment. *Proceedings of the survey research methods section of the ASA at JSM 1998* (pp. 41–49).

Couper, M. P. (2000). Web surveys: A review of issues and approaches. *Public Opinion Quarterly, 64*, 464–494.

Couper, M., & Wagner, J. (August 2011). Using paradata and responsive design to manage survey nonresponse. In *ISI World Statistics Congress, Dublin, Ireland.*

Cox, D. R. (1958). *Planning of experiments.* Wiley.

Cronbach, L. J. (1982). *Designing evaluations of educational and social programs.* San Francisco, CA: Jossey-Bass.

Dandurand, F., Shultz, T., & Onishi, K. (2008). Comparing online and lab methods in a problem-solving experiment. *Behavior Research Methods, 40*(2), 428–434.

Dean, A., Voss, D., & Draguljić, D. (2017). *Design and analysis of experiments* (2nd ed.). Berlin: Springer.

Deaton, A. (2010). Instruments, randomization, and learning about development. *Journal of Economic Literature, 48*(2), 424–455.

Dobrick, F. M., Fischer, J., & Hagen, L. M. (2018). *Research ethics in the digital age: Ethics for the social sciences and humanities in the times of mediatization and digitization. Wiesbaden*: Springer VS. https://doi.org/10.1007/978-3-658-12909-5

DuMouchel, W., & Jones, B. (1994). A simple Bayesian modification of D-optimal designs to reduce dependence on an assumed model. *Technometrics, 36*(1), 37–47. https://doi.org/10.2307/1269197

Eichhorn, J. (2021). *Survey research and sampling*. London: SAGE.

Eifler, S. (2010). Validity of a factorial survey approach to the analysis of criminal behavior. *Methodology: European Journal of Research Methods for the Behavioral and Social Sciences, 6*, 139–146.

Faber, L. G., Maurits, N. M., & Lorist, M. M. (2012). Mental fatigue affects visual selective attention. *PLoS ONE, 7*(10), e48073. https://doi.org/10.1371/journal.pone.0048073

Fielding, N., Lee, R. M., & Blank, G. (2017). *The sage handbook of online research methods* (2nd ed.). London: SAGE.

Finn, J. D., & Achilles, C. M. (1990). Answers and questions about class size: A statewide experiment. *American Educational Research Journal, 27*(3), 557–577.

Frankel, M. S., & Siang, S. (1999). *Ethical and legal aspects of human subjects research on the internet*. Washington, DC: American Association for the Advancement of Science.

Freeman, J. B., & Ambady, N. (2010). MouseTracker: Software for studying real-time mental processing using a computer mouse-tracking method. *Behavior Research Methods, 42*(1), 226–241.

Fricker, R. D., & Schonlau, M. (2002). Advantages and disadvantages of internet research surveys: Evidence from the literature. *Field Methods, 14*(4), 347–365.

Frith, J. (2015). *Smartphones as locative media*. Cambridge: Polity.

Gerber, A. S., & Green, D. P. (2012). *Field experiments: Design analysis and interpretation*. Norton & Co.

Gibson, J. J. (1977). The theory of affordances. In R. E. Shaw & J. Bransford (Eds.), *Perceiving, acting, and knowing*. Hillsdale, NJ: Lawrence Erlbaum.

Goldstein, N. J., & Hays, N. A. (2011). Illusory power transference: The vicarious experience of power. *Administrative Science Quarterly, 56*(4), 593–621.

Gosling, S. & Johnson, J. (Eds.). (2010). *Advanced internet methods in the behavioral sciences*. Washington, DC: American Psychological Association.

Goos, P. (2002). Optimal split-plot designs. In: *The optimal design of blocked and split-plot experiments. Lecture notes in statistics (Vol. 164)*. New York, NY: Springer. https://doi.org/10.1007/978-1-4613-0051-9_8

Gravenhorst, F., Muaremi, A., Bardram, J., Grünerbl, A., Mayora, O., Wurzer, G., Frost, M., Osmani, V., Arnrich, B., Lukowicz, P., et al. (2015). Mobile phones as medical devices in mental disorder treatment: An overview. *Personal and Ubiquitous Computing, 19*, 335–353.

Groves, R. M., Couper, M. P., Presser, S., Singer, E., Tourangeau, R., Acosta, G. P., & Nelson, L. (2006). Experiments in producing nonresponse bias. *International Journal of Public Opinion Quarterly, 70*(5), 720–736.

Groves, R. M., Singer, E., & Corning, A. (2000). Leverage-saliency theory of survey participation: Description and an illustration. *The Public Opinion Quarterly, 64*(3), 299–308.

Green, D. P., & Kern, H. L. (2012). Modeling heterogeneous treatment effects in survey experiments with Bayesian additive regression trees. *Public Opinion Quarterly, 76*(3), 491–511. https://doi.org/10.1093/poq/nfs036

Grünerbl, A., Muaremi, A., Osmani, V., Bahle, G., Öhler, S., Tröster, G., Mayora, O., Haring, C., & Lukowicz, P. (2015). Smartphone-based recognition of states and state changes in bipolar disorder patients. *IEEE Journal of Biomedical and Health Informatics, 19*, 140–148.

Gupta, S., Kohavi, R., Deng, A., Omhover, J., & Janowski, P. (May 2019). A/B testing at scale: Accelerating software innovation. In *Companion proceedings of the 2019 World Wide Web Conference* (pp. 1299–1300).

Hahl, O., & Zuckerman, E. W. (2014). The denigration of heroes? How the status attainment process shapes attributions of considerateness and authenticity. *American Journal of Sociology, 120*(2), 504–554.

Hamada, M. S., & Wu, C. F. J. (2009). *Experiments: planning analysis and optimization* (2nd ed.). John Wiley and Sons.

Han, M., Bang, J. H., Nugent, C., McClean, S., & Lee, S. (2014). A lightweight hierarchical activity recognition framework using smartphone sensors. *Sensors, 14*, 16181–16195.

Han, M., Vinh, L. T., Lee, Y. K., & Lee, S. (2012). Comprehensive context recognizer based on multimodal sensors in a smartphone. *Sensors, 12*, 12588–12605.

Hand, D. J., & Vinciotti, V. (2003). Local versus global models for classification problems: Fitting models where it matters. *The American Statistician, 57*(2), 124–131.

Harrison, G., & List, J. (2004). Field experiments. *Journal of Economic Literature, 42*, 1013–1059.

Heerwegh, D. (2003). Explaining response latencies and changing answers using client-side paradata from a web survey. *Social Science Computer Review, 21*, 360–373.

Historical trends and future directions. In M. Delli Carpini, L. Huddy, & R. Shapiro (Eds.), Research in micropolitics. Greenwood, CA: JAI Press.

Howitt, D., & Cramer, D. (2011). *Introduction to research methods in psychology.* Harlow: Pearson Education.

Hunzaker, M. B. F. (2017). *Cultural cognition and bias in information transmission.* Doctoral dissertation.

Hur, T., Bang, J., Kim, D., Banos, O., & Lee, S. (2017). Smartphone location-independent physical activity recognition based on transportation natural vibration analysis. *Sensors, 17*, 931.

Jackob, N., Arens, J., & Zerback, T. (2005). Sampling procedure, questionnaire design, online implementation, and survey response in a multi- national online journalist survey. *Paper presented at the joint WAPOR/ISSC Conference:*

Conducting international social surveys. cissris.org/uploadi/editor/
1132070316WAPORPaper.pdf. Accessed on October 20, 2022.

Jagoda, P. (2021). *Experimental games. Critique play and design in the age of gamification.* Chicago, IL: University of Chicago Press.

Johnson, A., Mulder, B., Sijbinga, A., & Hulsebos, L. (2012). Action as a window to perception: Measuring attention with mouse movements. *Applied Cognitive Psychology, 26,* 802–809.

Jones, B., Lin, D. K. J., & Nachtsheim, C. J. (2008). Bayesian D-optimal supersaturated designs. *Journal of Statistical Planning and Inference, 138*(1), 86–92. https://doi.org/10.1016/j.jspi.2007.05.021

Kahneman, D., & Tversky, A. (2008). *Choices, values, and frames.* Cambridge: Cambridge University Press.

Kaplowitz, M. D., Hadlock, T. D., & Levine, R. (2004). A comparison of web and mail survey response rates. *Public Opinion Quarterly, 68,* 94–101.

Kiesler, C. A., Collins, B. E., & Miller, N. (1969). *Attitude change.* New York, NY: Wiley.

Kirk, R. E. (1995). *Experimental design: Procedures for the behavioral sciences* (3rd ed.). Pacific Grove, CA: Brooks/Cole.

Kramer, A. D. I., Guillory, J. E., & Hancock, J. T. (2014). Experimental evidence of massive-scale emotional contagion through social networks. *Proceedings of the National Academy of Sciences, 111*(24), 8788–8790.

Kraut, R., Olson, J., Banaji, M., Bruckman, A., Cohen, J., & Couper, M. (2004). Psychological research online: Report of board of scientific affairs' advisory group on the conduct of research on the internet. *American Psychologist, 59,* 105–117.

Lane, N. D., Lin, M., Mohammod, M., Yang, X., Lu, H., Cardone, G., Ali, S., Doryab, A., Berke, E., Campbell, A. T., et al. (2014). BeWell: Sensing sleep, physical activities and social interactions to promote wellbeing. *Mobile Networks and Applications, 19,* 345–359.

Lohr, S. L. (2021). *Sampling: Design and analysis* (3rd ed.). Chapman and Hall/CRC.

Lomranz, J., Bergman, S., Eyal, N., & Shmotkin, D. (1998). Indoor and outdoor activities of aged women and men as related to depression and well-being. *The International Journal of Aging and Human Development, 26,* 303–314.

Louviere, J., Hensher, D., & Swait, J. (2000). *Stated choice methods: Analysis and application.* New York, NY: Cambridge University Press.

Madden, T. J., Hewett, K., & Roth, M. S. (2000). Managing images in different cultures: A cross-national study of color meanings and preferences. *Journal of International Marketing, 8*(4), 90–107.

Martín, H., Bernardos, A. M., Iglesias, J., & Casar, J. R. (2013). Activity logging using lightweight classification techniques in mobile devices. *Personal and Ubiquitous Computing, 17,* 675–695.

Martin, J. L. (2011). *The explanation of social action.* Oxford: Oxford University Press.

Mathy, R. M., Kerr, D. L., & Haydin, B. M. (2003). Methodological rigor and ethical considerations in Internet-mediated research. *Psychotherapy: Theory, Research, Practice, Training, 40,* 77–85.

McCabe, S. E. (2004). Comparison of web and mail surveys in collecting illicit drug use data: A randomized experiment. *Journal of Drug Education, 34,* 61–72.

McFadden, D. (1974). Conditional logit analysis of qualitative choice behaviour. In P. Zarembka (Ed.), *Frontiers in econometrics* (pp. 105–142). New York, NY: Academic Press.

McFadden, D. (1986). The choice theory approach to market research. *Marketing Science, 5*, 275–279.

McFadden, D., & Train, K. (2000). Mixed MNL models for discrete response. *Journal of Applied Econometrics, 15*(15), 447–470.

McGraw, K. M., & Hoekstra, V. (1994). Experimentation in political science: Historical trends and future directions. *Research in Micropolitics, 4*, 3–29.

Milkman, K. L., Gromet, D., Ho, H., Kay, J. S., Lee, T. W., Pandiloski, P., Park, Y., Rai, A., Bazerman, M., Beshears, J., Bonacorsi, L., Camerer, C., Chang, E., Chapman, G., Cialdini, R., Dai, H., Eskreis-Winkler, L., Fishbach, A., Gross, J. J., … Duckworth, A. L. (2021). Megastudies improve the impact of applied behavioural science. *Nature, 600*(7889), 478–483. https://doi.org/10.1038/s41586-021-04128-4

Moles, K., Atkinson, P., Delamont, S., Cernat, A., Sakshaug, J. W., & Williams, R. A. (2020). *Mobile methods*. SAGE Publications. https://methods.sagepub.com/foundations/mobile-methods

Montgomery, D. C. (2009). *Introduction to statistical quality control*. Chichester: John Wiley & Sons Incorporated.

Moturu, S. T., Khayal, I., Aharony, N., Pan, W., & Pentland, A. (2011). *Using social sensing to understand the links between sleep, mood, and sociability. In proceedings of the 2011 IEEE international conference on privacy, security, risk and trust and IEEE international conference on social computing, PASSAT/ SocialCom 2011, Boston, MA, USA, 9–11 October 2011*, pp. 208–214.

Muaremi, A., Seiter, J., Bexheti, A., & Tröster, G. (2013). Monitor andunderstand pilgrims: Data collection using smartphones and wearable devices. *Proc ACM Ubiquitous Computing (UbiComp), HASCA Workshop, 2013*. https://www.researchgate.net/publication/263651653_Monitoring_the_Impact_of_Stress_on_the_Sleep_Patterns_of_Pilgrims_using_Wearable_Sensors.

Nederhof, A. J. (1985). Methods of coping with social desirability bias: A review. *European Journal of Social Psychology, 15*, 263–280.

Neisser, U. (1976). *Cognition and reality*. San Francisco, CA: Freeman.

Neyman, J. (1923). On the application of probability theory to agricultural experiments. Essay on principles. *Statistical Science, 5*(4), 465–480.

Norberg, P. A., Horne, D. R., & Horne, D. A. (2007). The privacy paradox: Personal information disclosure intentions versus behaviors. *Journal of Consumer Affairs, 41*(1), 100–126.

Norman, D. A. (1999). Affordance, conventions, and design. *Interactions, 6*, 38–41.

Norman, K. L., Friedman, Z., Norman, K., & Stevenson, R. (2001). Navigational issues in the design of online self-administered questionnaires. *Behaviour & Information Technology, 20*(1), 37–45.

Ong, D., & Wang, J. (2015). Income attraction: An online dating field experiment. *Journal of Economic Behavior and Organization, 111*, 13–22.

Parker, S. W., & Todd, P. E. (2017). Conditional cash transfers: The case of Progresa/ Oportunidades. *Journal of Economic Literature, 55*(3), 866–915.

Parigi, P., Santana, J. J., & Cook, K. S. (2017). Online field experiments: Studying social interactions in context. *Social Psychology Quarterly*, *80*(1), 1–19.

Parsons, T. D. (2019). *Ethical challenges in digital psychology and cyberpsychology* (1st ed.). Cambridge: Cambridge University Press.

Payne, B. K., & Gawronski, B. (Eds.). (2010). *Handbook of implicit cognition: Measurement theory and applications*. New York, NY: Guilford Press.

Pearl, J., & Bareinboim, E. (2014). External validity: From do-calculus to transportability across populations. *Statistical Science*, *29*(4), 579–595.

Petzold, K., & Wolbring, T. (2019). What can we learn from factorial surveys about human behavior? A validation study comparing field and survey experiments on discrimination. *Methodology*, *15*, 19–30.

Peytchev, A., Couper, M. P., McCabe, S. E., & Crawford, S. D. (2006). Web survey design: Paging versus scrolling. *International Journal of Public Opinion Quarterly*, *70*(4), 596–607.

Reeves, B., Cummings, J. J., Scarborough, J. K., & Yeykelis, L. (2015). Increasing energy efficiency with entertainment media: An experimental and field test of the influence of a social game on performance of energy behaviors. *Environment and Behavior*, *47*(1), 102–115. https://doi.org/10.1177/0013916513506442

Reips, U.-D. (1997). Das psychologische experimentieren im Internet [Psychological experimenting on the Internet]. In B. Batinic (Ed.), *Internet für Psychologen* (pp. 245–265). Göttingen: Hogrefe.

Reips, U. D. (2000). The web experiment method: Advantages, disadvantages, and solutions. In M. Birnbaum (Ed.), *Psychological experiments on the internet*. San Diego, CA: Academic Press.

Reips, U. D. (2002a). Theory and techniques of conducting web experiments. In B. Batinic, U. Reips, & M. Bosnjak (Eds.), *Online social sciences*. Seattle, WA: Hogrefe and Huber.

Reips, U. D. (2002b). Standards for internet-based experimenting. *Journal of Experimental Psychology*, *49*(4), 243–256.

Reips, U. D., & Krantz, J. (2010). Conducting true experiments on the web. In S. Gosling & J. Johnson (Eds.), *Advanced internet methods in the behavioral sciences*. Washington, DC: American Psychological Association.

Reuben, E., Sapienza, P., & Zingales, L. (2014). How stereotypes impair women's careers in science. *Proceedings of the National Academy of Sciences*, *111*(12), 4403–4408. https://doi.org/10.1073/pnas.1314788111

Rubin, D. B. (1974). Estimating causal effects of treatments in randomized and non-randomized studies. *Journal of Educational Psychology*, *66*(5), 688–701.

Sarsons, H., Gërxhani, K., Reuben, E., & Schram, A. (2021). Gender differences in recognition for group work. *Journal of Political Economy*, *129*, 101–147.

Scheidt, R. (1981). Ecologically-valid inquiry: Fait accompli? *Human Development*, *24*, 225–228.

Schmidt, C., Collette, F., Cajochen, C., & Peigneux, P. (2007). A time to think: Circadian rhythms in human cognition. *Cognitive Neuropsychology*, *24*, 755–789.

Schoemann, M., O'Hora, D., Dale, R., & Scherbaum, S. (2021). Using mouse cursor tracking to investigate online cognition: Preserving methodological ingenuity while moving toward reproducible science. *Psychonomic Bulletin & Review*, *28*(3), 766–787. https://doi.org/10.3758/s13423-020-01851-3

Shadish, W., Cook, T., & Campbell, D. (2002). *Experimental and quasi experimental designs for generalized causal inference*. Boston, MA: Houghton Mifflin.

Shamon, H., & Berning, C. C. (2020). Attention check items and instructions in online surveys: Boon or bane for data quality? *Survey Research Methods*, 55–77. https://doi.org/10.18148/SRM/2020.V14I1.7374

Simon, H. A. (1954). Spurious correlation: A causal interpretation. *Journal of the American Statistical Association*, *49*(267), 467–492. https://doi.org/10.2307/2281124

Sobel, M. E. (1995). Causal inference in the social and behavioral sciences. In G. Arminger, C. C. Clogg, & M. E. Sobel (Eds.), *Handbook of statistical modeling for the social and behavioral sciences*. Boston, MA: Springer.

Song, H., & Schwarz, N. (2008). If it's hard to read, it's hard to do: Processing fluency affects effort prediction and motivation. *Psychological Science*, *19*(10), 986–988.

Spottswood, E., & Hancock, J. T. (2016). The positivity bias and prosocial deception on Facebook. *Computers in Human Behavior*, *65*, 252–259.

Stanton, J. M., & Rogelberg, S. G. (2001). Using Internet/Intranet web pages to collect organizational research data. *Organizational Research Methods*, *4*, 200–217.

Steinert, J., Sterneberg, H., Prince, H., Fasolo, B., Galizzi, M. M., Buthe, T., & Veltri, G. A. (2022). COVID-19 vaccine hesitancy in eight European countries: Prevalence, determinants, and heterogeneity. *Science Advances*, *8* (17), eabm9825. https://doi.org/10.1126/sciadv.abm9825

Stieger, S., & Reips, U. D. (2010). What are participants doing while filling in an online questionnaire: A paradata collection tool and an empirical study. *Computers in Human Behavior*, *26*(6), 1488–1495.

Stieglitz, S., Lattemann, C., Robra-Bissantz, S., Zarnekow, R., & Brockmann, T. (2017). *Gamification using game elements in serious contexts*. Springer International Publishing.

Stutzman, F., Gross, R., & Acquisti, A. (2013). Silent listeners: The evolution of privacy and disclosure on Facebook. *Journal of Privacy and Confidentiality*, *4*(2).

Taback, N. (2022). *Design and analysis of experiments and observational studies using R*. Chapman & Hall/CRC.

Thurstone, L. L. (1927). A law of comparative judgment. *Psychological Review*, *34*, 273–286.

Toepoel, V. (2016). *Doing surveys online*. London: SAGE.

Toplak, M. E., West, R. F., & Stanovich, K. E. (2014). Assessing miserly information processing: An expansion of the cognitive reflection test. *Thinking & Reasoning*, *20*(2), 147–168.

Torous, J., Kiang, M. V., Lorme, J., & Onnela, J. P. (2016). New tools for new research in psychiatry: A scalable and customizable platform to empower data driven smartphone research. *JMIR Mental Health*, *3*, e16.

Tourangeau, R., Conrad, F. G., & Couper, M. P. (2013). *The science of web surveys*. Oxford University Press.

Tourangeau, R., Couper, M. P., & Conrad, F. (2004). Spacing, position, and order: Interpretive heuristics for visual features of survey questions. *Public Opinion Quarterly*, *68*(3), 368–393.

van Dongen, H. P., & Dinges, D. F. (2005). Sleep, circadian rhythms, and psychomotor vigilance. *Clinical Journal of Sport Medicine*, *24*, 237–249.

Vanello, N., Guidi, A., Gentili, C., Werner, S., Bertschy, G., Valenza, G., Lanata, A., & Scilingo, E. P. (2012). Speech analysis for mood state characterization in bipolar patients. *Conference Proceedings IEEE Engineering in Medicine and Biology Society*, *2012*, 2104–2107.

Veltri, G. A. (2019). *Digital social research* (p. 224). Cambridge: Polity. ISBN: 9781509529308.

Veltri, G. A., & Ivchenko, A. (2017). The impact of different forms of cognitive scarcity on online privacy disclosure. *Computers in Human Behavior*, *73*, 238–246.

Veltri, G. A., Lupiáñez-Villanueva, F., Folkvord, F., Theben, A., & Gaskell, G. (2023). The impact of online platform transparency of information on consumers' choices. *Behavioural Public Policy*, *7*(1), 55–82.

Veltri, G. A., Steinert, J. I., Sternberg, H., Galizzi, M., Fasolo, B., Kourtidis, P., Büthe, T., & Gaskell, G. (2023b). *Assessing the perceived effect of non-pharmaceutical interventions on SARS-Cov-2 transmission risk: Evidence from a large discrete choice experiment in 6 European countries*. Unpublished manuscript.

Wager, S., & Athey, S. (2018). Estimation and inference of heterogeneous treatment effects using random forests. *Journal of the American Statistical Association*, *113*(523), 1228–1242.

Wagner, J. R. (2008). *Adaptive survey design to reduce nonresponse bias*. Doctoral dissertation, University of Michigan.

Wason, K., Polonsky, M., & Hyman, M. (2002). Designing vignette studies in marketing. *Australasian Marketing Journal*, *10*, 41–58.

Watts, D. J. (2014). Common sense and sociological explanations. *American Journal of Sociology*, *120*(2), 313–351. https://doi.org/10.1086/678271

Webb, E. J., Campbell, D. T., Schwartz, R. D., & Sechrest, L. (1966). *Unobtrusive measures*. Chicago, IL: Rand McNally.

Weller, L., & Livingston, R. (1988). Effect of color of questionnaire on emotional responses. *The Journal of General Psychology*, *115*(4), 433–440.

Wenz, A. (2021). Do distractions during web survey completion affect data quality? Findings from a laboratory experiment. *Social Science Computer Review*, *39*(1), 148–161. https://doi.org/10.1177/0894439319851503

Wierzbicka, A. (1992). *Semantics, culture, and cognition: Universal human concepts in culture-specific configurations*. Oxford University Press.

Wittenbrink, B., & Schwarz, N. (2007). *Implicit measures of attitudes*. Guilford.

Wohlfahrt-Laymann, J., Hermens, H., Villalonga, C., Vollenbroek-Hutten, M., & Banos, O. (2018). MobileCogniTracker. *Journal of Ambient Intelligence and Humanized Computing*, *1868–5145*, 1–8.

Woodward, J. (2000). Explanation and invariance in the special sciences. *British Journal for the Philosophy of Science*, *51*, 221–222.

Woodward, J. F. (2003). *Making things happen: A theory of causal explanation*. Oxford University Press.

Woodward, J. (2005). *Making things happen: A theory of causal explanation*. Oxford: Oxford University Press.

Xinkun Nie, X., & Wager, S. (2017). *Quasi-Oracle estimation of heterogeneous treatment effects*. Papers 1712.04912, arXiv.org, revised August 2020.

Xu, K., Qi, G., Huang, J., Wu, T., & Fu, X. (2018). Detecting bursts in sentiment-aware topics from social media. *Knowledge-Based Systems, 141*, 44–54.

Yan, T., & Tourangeau, R. (2008). Fast times and easy questions: The effects of age, experience and question complexity on web survey response times. *Applied Cognitive Psychology: The Official Journal of the Society for Applied Research in Memory and Cognition, 22*(1), 51–68.

Yang, F., & Yao, Z. (2022). *Travel behavior characteristics analysis technology based on mobile phone location data: Methodology and empirical research*. Shanghai: Tongji University Press.

Yule, G. U. (1896). On the correlation of total pauperism with proportion of out-relief ii: Males over 65. *Economic Journal, 6*, 613–623.

Zeileis, A., & Hornik, K. (2007). Generalized M-fluctuation tests for parameter instability. *Statistica Neerlandica, 61*(4), 488–508.

Zhang, C., & Conrad, F. (July 2014). Speeding in web surveys: The tendency to answer very fast and its association with straightlining. In *Survey Research Methods, 8*(2), 127–135.

Zimmer, M. & Kinder-Kurlanda, K. (Eds.). (2017). *Internet research ethics for the social age: New challenges, cases, and contexts*. Lang Publishing.

Zwerina, K. (2000). *Discrete choice experiments in marketing: Use of priors in efficient choice designs and their application to individual preference measurement* (2nd ed.). Heidelberg: Physica.

INDEX